MIRACLES NOW

ALSO BY GABRIELLE BERNSTEIN

Books

Add More ~ing to Your Life

May Cause Miracles

Spirit Junkie

CDs/DVDs

God Is My Publicist*

May Cause Miracles Guided Meditation Album

MediDating*

*Available from Hay House

Please visit:

Hay House USA: www.hayhouse.com®
Hay House Australia: www.hayhouse.com.au
Hay House UK: www.hayhouse.co.uk
Hay House South Africa: www.hayhouse.co.za
Hay House India: www.hayhouse.co.in

MIRACLES NOW

108 Life-Changing Tools for Less Stress,
More Flow, and Finding Your True Purpose

GABRIELLE BERNSTEIN

HAY HOUSE, INC.
Carlsbad, California • New York City
London • Sydney • Johannesburg
Vancouver • Hong Kong • New Delhi

Published and distributed in the United States by: Hay House, Inc.: www.hayhouse.com® • **Published and distributed in Australia by:** Hay House Australia Pty. Ltd.: www.hayhouse.com.au • **Published and distributed in the United Kingdom by:** Hay House UK, Ltd.: www.hayhouse.co.uk • **Published and distributed in the Republic of South Africa by:** Hay House SA (Pty), Ltd.: www.hayhouse.co.za • **Distributed in Canada by:** Raincoast Books: www.raincoast.com • **Published in India by:** Hay House Publishers India: www.hayhouse.co.in

Cover design: Emily French • *Cover photo:* Chloe Crespi • *Interior design:* Pamela Homan • *Interior photos:* Chloe Crespi, Michael O'Neill, Katrina Sorrentino • *Tapping Points illustration:* Courtesy of Nick Ortner

Library of Congress Cataloging-in-Publication Data

Bernstein, Gabrielle.
  Miracles now : 108 life-changing tools for less stress, more flow, and finding your true purpose / Gabrielle Bernstein. -- 1st edition.
    pages cm
  ISBN 978-1-4019-4434-6 (hardback)
  1. Attitude change. 2. Self-actualization (Psychology) 3. Self-realization. 4. Course in Miracles. I. Title.
  BF327.B473 2014
  155.9'042--dc23

                              2013038725

Tradepaper ISBN: 978-1-4019-4433-9

10 9 8 7 6 5 4 3 2 1
1st edition, April 2014
2nd edition, April 2015

Printed in the United States of America

To my great spiritual teachers, Marianne Williamson and Gurmukh Kaur Khalsa.

Thank you for reminding me that the light I see in you is a reflection of my own light.

Contents

Introduction

I do not believe in miracles. I rely on them.

— YOGI BHAJAN

Over the last several years, our collective negativity and fear have adversely affected the economy, the environment, and the health of all beings on this planet. Due to new technology, global warming, financial crises, violent crimes, political turmoil, and planetary shifts, we've become more sensitive to the energy around us and the pace of life. The world has sped up, and the changes we're experiencing can be difficult to navigate. The intensity of this time can be very uncomfortable and, in many cases, paralyzing. Without clear direction, people can feel misaligned with their purpose, their relationships, and their overall connection to the world.

Right now we're in a special and powerful position, because the world is having a spiritual awakening. When energy speeds up there is no space for playing small, and nothing can remain hidden. At some point all lies are brought to the surface and truth comes forth no matter how hard we try to hide it. Cynics are filling the yoga studios and the spiritual choir is growing larger. There is a massive call for more lightworkers, and now is our time to rise up and bring more positivity to the world. When the masses begin to vibrate with an energy of love, the world will no longer be a container for war, violence, and lies.

This book will set you on the right path and help you release fear and tension to bust through your blocks fast. In this day and age we need ways to clear our stress and fear quickly because you simply might not have time to do an hour of yoga each day or sit in meditation for 30 minutes whenever anxiety creeps in. Having tools for creating fast shifts is imperative.

This book offers soulful methods for achieving peace drawn from some of the world's greatest spiritual teachings. What's unique about the techniques I've chosen is that you can use them to quickly clear your stress and fear any time—even if you only have a minute to spare. Let's get honest: We're overwhelmed enough. Our spiritual practice can't add to that sense of overwhelm. Instead, our practice must be designed to bust through the stress and feelings of being overwhelmed fast so we can live with ease. This book is like a juggernaut for eliminating stress.

Miracles Now contains 108 techniques for the most common problems we face. Each technique will highlight the issue, then offer up spiritual principles, meditations, and practical, do-them-now tools. I will break down each technique in an easy-to-digest way, while incorporating powerful spiritual truths, life-changing Kundalini meditations, and lessons and principles from the metaphysical text *A Course in Miracles*.

As a student and teacher of *A Course in Miracles* and Kundalini yoga and meditation, it has become my mission to translate these life-changing spiritual truths for all seekers. *A Course in Miracles* is a metaphysical self-taught curriculum based on the principle that when we choose love over fear we experience miraculous change. The *Course* emphasizes the practice of turning our fears over to the care of our inner guide and places strong emphasis on forgiveness. The *Course* teaches us that through the experience of forgiveness we will know true peace.

Kundalini is the yoga of awareness, which focuses on enhancing one's intuition and strengthening the energy field. Kundalini aims to draw forth the creative potential of an individual to have strong values, be truthful, and focus on compassion and consciousness. Kundalini was brought to the West in 1969 by Yogi Bhajan, a yoga master. Yogi Bhajan brought these teachings knowing we would need the Kundalini technology to balance the energy of what was to come. In the seventies Yogi Bhajan prophesized that these times would be tumultuous. In reference to these times he said, "The capacity of the mind will reach its optimum in order to deal with everyday life. The world will become smaller and smaller and smaller. So man's vitality has to become larger and larger and larger." He felt it was his mission to give us the tools to calm our nervous system, restore our energy, and cultivate compassion.

It is a great honor to share the principles of both *A Course in Miracles* and Kundalini throughout this book. These tools will help you release all that blocks your connection to your inner power. When you practice these techniques, fear will melt away, inspiration will spring up, and a sense of peace will set in. Most important, you will build a relationship to the power within you—and this power connection is essential. The power I speak of is your connection to love. The more we tune into our own frequency of love, the more love will spread. When love is the trend there is no room for violence and war. Trust me when I say: Your practice is crucial in the awakening of the world. Each person's energy matters.

There is another reason these techniques are so important, and it goes beyond ourselves: As we release stress in our lives, we help others do the same. Think about it. When you walk into a room and you're totally stressed out, you immediately bring down the energy—your friends, family, co-workers, even strangers can sense your tension and become uncomfortable. But when you enter a space calm and peaceful, you exude grace and ease. That grace is immediately bestowed upon everyone around you, even if they don't realize it on a conscious level.

Your energy has far more power than you can even imagine. There is energy in your spoken words, in your e-mails, and in your physical presence. When we function from a fearful, low-level energetic state, our thoughts and energy can literally pollute the world. Conversely, when we function from a place of positive energy, the world around us becomes more positive. The truth is that fear cannot coexist with love. Therefore, we must learn how to dissolve all boundaries with love by taking responsibility for our own energy. In doing so, we'll raise the energy around us.

To make this practice even more radical, I've set you up to be the miracle messenger. *A Course in Miracles* teaches that when two or more people are gathered in the name of love, a miracle occurs. Therefore, as you use these techniques, you'll be guided to share them. Each daily practice has been boiled down to a 140-character explanation. (And I *know* you can handle 140 characters.) If you dig it, share it. You can tweet the message, pin it, post it to Facebook, or pass it along on Instagram. Each Miracle Message will end with the hashtag #MiraclesNow. The intention for using the hashtag is to make sure your tweets begin to trend. There is no greater trend than the trend of love. When you are inspired, it's important to share the message. *(E-book readers can share from their reader.)*

My hope and my intention is to arm you with radical spiritual principles, transformational meditations, and mindful practices that will help you rise to your highest capacity, experience a more joyful life, and serve in a greater way. There is a massive payoff to following this plan: You will feel awesome! Your bucket list will become your reality, and you'll live a life beyond your wildest dreams. Putting simple techniques into action every day is extremely powerful—because miracles arise from new patterns and shifts in your perception.

Practice these principles and you'll quickly move through any pain that has been holding you back and make space to have a richer experience. And I'm talking about every aspect of your life: your relationships, your work and money, your health, your sense of self, and so on. Most important, you'll have a toolbox of spiritual techniques for navigating the wild energy of this time.

The best way to begin this journey is to be open to each technique regardless of your initial reaction to it. My hope is that you try each one at least once. Give yourself the chance to be surprised. Then you can decide which tools are best for you. Even if you only regularly apply one of these tools in your life, you will experience miraculous shifts.

Now, let's get this miracle train on the tracks and start busting through your blocks, releasing anxiety, and living a fearless life. Let's begin creating Miracles Now.

#1: HAPPINESS IS A CHOICE YOU MAKE.

Whenever I'm asked about the greatest lesson I've learned, my response is: *Happiness is a choice I make.* It's very easy to look for happiness outside ourselves: in a relationship, a dream job, or the perfect body weight. When we chase happiness externally, we're simply looking for God in all the wrong places. The outside search is based on false projections we place on the world. These projections build up a wall against true happiness, which lies within us. This first exercise will help you understand how nothing "out there" can save you from the conflict that resides within. You must develop a rich inner life to enjoy life altogether.

Each time we make this shift and choose happiness, we experience a miracle. Our mind shifts from fearful delusions and reconnects to our truth, which is love. Creating these shifts requires a dedicated commitment to choosing love. To begin your commitment to new perceptions, start by paying attention to attack thoughts toward yourself and others. Whenever you notice your thoughts detour into attack mode, say out loud or to yourself: *Happiness is a choice I make.* Make this your mantra.

The more you retrain yourself to choose happiness over fear, the more blissful you will be. Repeating a new behavior is what makes change stick. When you repeat a new pattern often, you literally change the neural pathways in your brain. This shift helps true change settle in.

Happiness is your choice. You can choose today.

Now it's time to spread the love! Tweet, Facebook, pin, Instagram, e-mail, and repeat the Miracle Message below. Pay it forward by carrying the message.

Miracle Message #1:

Happiness is a choice I make.

#MiraclesNow

#2: CLEAN UP YOUR SIDE OF THE STREET.

If you want to live a miraculous life, you must be willing to look at your behavior and take responsibility for the life you've created up until now. The first technique helped you understand that happiness is a choice. Now it's time to deepen this understanding by witnessing how you've chosen fear over happiness.

This practice will help you become the nonjudgmental witness of your fears. Make a list of your top ten biggest fears. As you look closely at these fears, get honest about how they've dominated your life. See how your thoughts have created your reality.

Then, next to each fear, write down the reason you believe this fear to be true. Write as little or as much as you desire. There's only one rule: Get honest. You may find that your fear is based on an experience from your past that you've been replaying over and over for decades. Or you may come to see how your fear is based on a future event that hasn't even happened. As you look at your fears head-on, you'll begin to see how much of what you fear is just False Evidence Appearing Real. When you act on this false evidence, you create chaos in your life.

This practice will guide you to focus more on your side of the street and take responsibility for the world you see. This exercise brings up a lot of funky feelings and can be hard at first. With this in mind, I will arm you with a beautiful prayer from *A Course in Miracles*. Whenever you feel overwhelmed by your fears, simply recite this prayer out loud, surrender, and allow healing to set in:

Take this from me and look upon it, judging it for me.

Teach me how not to make of it an obstacle to peace.

Now it's your turn to remind others to look closely at their fears. Start planting the seed of positivity with today's Miracle Message.

Miracle Message #2:

**I choose to reinterpret my fears with
a more loving perspective.**

#MiraclesNow

#3: TO FEEL SUPPORTED, SUPPORT YOURSELF.

During my lectures and workshops I often hear people complain that they're not feeling supported by others. They might be upset with their work colleagues, families, or friends, but whatever the circumstances, they've all slipped into victim mode by resenting others for their lack of support. Rather than commiserate with these folks, I flash the universal mirror at them and ask, "Are you supporting yourself?" Typically they respond with a weepy reply of "No, I'm not."

You see, the way we experience the world around us is a direct reflection of the world within us. If our thoughts and energy are not supportive, then our life won't be supported. Therefore, we must take responsibility by consciously supporting ourselves in every given moment.

Whenever you're in a time of need and feel unsupported or alone, immediately ask yourself, "How can I support myself more?" Then take action. Simple right actions toward self-support can greatly change your attitude and experience. Say something kind to yourself, consciously think an empowering thought about yourself, or ask someone for help.

We often think that people should be able to read our minds and simply "know" when we need support, but they can't. The people in our lives have their own struggles and challenges, and they may not see ours, especially if we appear to be holding it together. Ultimately, asking for help is a radical act of self-support. One of the biggest ways we don't support ourselves is by not asking for support. Asking can take courage, but the reward is immense. Not only will you receive the support you need, you'll deepen your relationship with whomever you're asking.

These small right actions can greatly enhance your life in an instant. Making the simple shift from a power-less victim to a strong person who can care for yourself can change your life forever.

Miracle Message #3:

If I want to feel supported, I must support myself.

#MiraclesNow

#4: PEACE IS IN YOUR PULSE.

Everyday life brings challenges and discomfort, which can knock us out of a peaceful place. Throughout this book, one key principle for releasing stress and achieving peace I'll recommend again and again is meditation.

Many people want to meditate but don't know where to begin. They are aware of the benefits and possibly have enjoyed some mindful moments, but have had trouble making meditation a daily practice. One obstacle can be the fact that many folks find meditation intimidating. They think they have to be masters right away to reap the rewards—but in truth, it's called a "practice" for a reason. Would you expect to play tennis like Serena Williams the first time you pick up a racquet? Of course not! But that doesn't mean you can't hit the court with focus and enthusiasm, get a great workout, and improve your skills. The same is true of meditation—even rookies can revel in the results immediately!

An easy way to begin meditation and access peace is through your pulse. Just by meditating on your own pulse, you can calm your mind, balance your brain hemispheres, and recalibrate your nervous system. This Kundalini meditation is called Learning to Meditate—clearly, it's the perfect place to start. If you're a newbie meditator, follow this practice and you'll be Zenned out in no time.

Through this simple meditation you can develop your ability to concentrate. It will also help you control your reactions in all situations and bring calm to even the most scattered mind.

Learning to Meditate

Sit in Easy Pose (comfortably cross-legged on the floor) with a slight neck lock, which means your chin is slightly down and your neck is straight.

Lightly close your eyes and focus on the space between your eyebrows (the third-eye point).

The mantra is *Sat Nam* (which means "truth identified").

The hand position (mudra) is simple. Place the four fingers of your right hand on your left wrist and feel your pulse. The fingers are in a straight line, lightly pressed on the wrist so you can feel your pulse in each fingertip. On each beat of your pulse, mentally hear the sound of *Sat Nam*.

This meditation is suggested for 11 minutes, but you can experience great benefits in just one minute. Practice this meditation daily to develop your intuition and calm your mind.

Miracle Message #4:

Peace is in your pulse.

#MiraclesNow

#5: WHY AM I TALKING?

Ever walk away from a conversation feeling hungover from all you said? Do you ever lose track of your filter and overshare? Or are you totally unable to listen to other people because you tend to ramble on about yourself?

Whenever you notice yourself oversharing, simply say to yourself, "W.A.I.T.: Why Am I Talking?" This simple acronym will take you out of the ego behavior and back into your truth. Even if you're mid-sentence, it's okay to W.A.I.T. Use this technique as often as possible and soon you'll also become a great listener!

I'm confident that today's Miracle Message will be well received. Simply share the following.

Miracle Message #5:

When you've overshared, simply say, "W.A.I.T.: Why am I talking?"

#MiraclesNow

#6: PEACE BEGINS WITH YOU.

No matter how happy or serene we may be, there are always those friends, family members, or co-workers who can get under our skin. Rather than allow these people to shake up your world, it's important to understand that they are your greatest assignments for spiritual growth.

Today's technique is a fantastic Kundalini meditation that offers you a fast, simple, and effective solution for releasing anger when people piss you off. You can practice this meditation anytime and anywhere. You can even begin right now.

Gently press your thumb against your index finger, then your middle finger, then your ring finger, then your pinkie finger.

When you touch your index finger, say: PEACE

When you touch your middle finger, say: BEGINS

When you touch your ring finger, say: WITH

When you touch your pinkie finger, say: ME

Breathe deeply as you say each word. Go as slow or as fast as you'd like. Use this technique in line at the bank, under the desk in an office meeting, or in the middle of a fight with your lover. This technique will get you through all kinds of crazy emotions and help you release resentment fast.

Now it's time to share the love. Post this Miracle Message and inspire others to see their relationships as assignments.

Miracle Message #6:

Relationships are assignments for
optimal growth and healing.

#MiraclesNow

#7: "THE MIRACLE COMES QUIETLY."

In this exercise you will be guided to understand the following message from the *Course*: "The miracle comes quietly into the mind that stops an instant and is still." Being still does not come easily for most people. When we're caught up in the chaos of insistent thoughts, we block our connection to the intuitive voice of guidance within. Much of our anxiety and stress comes when we're focused on fear and disconnected from the voice of our inner guide. The key to releasing that tension is to center back into stillness to realign with a natural state of peace. Having the tools to still our mind is imperative if we want to live a miraculous life guided by intuition rather than fear.

If you suffer from anxiety, today's technique is wonderful for releasing it. The simple steps outlined below are based on a Kundalini meditation for releasing anxiety and tension. Follow these steps and enjoy the stillness you will receive.

Step 1: Sit comfortably on a chair and bring both feet flat onto the floor.

Step 2: Close your mouth and roll your tongue clockwise, pushing it against the front of your mouth. Do this for 30 to 90 seconds.

Step 3: Reverse the direction and do it for the same amount of time.

Step 4: Sit for one minute of stillness.

This practice will guide you into a state of stillness. And it is in this stillness that you will feel anxiety subside as you deepen your connection to your inner guide. You'll come to learn that stillness can be our most powerful tool.

For this miracle message, you can share the quote from *A Course in Miracles.*

Miracle Message #7:

"The miracle comes quietly into the mind that stops an instant and is still."

#ACIM #MiraclesNow

#8: POSITIVE-PERCEPTION
PLAYLISTS
ARE POWERFUL.

Have you ever had a strong emotional reaction to a song? You know—the kind that makes tears well up in your eyes and goose bumps dot your skin as you're energized and inspired by the sound. If you have, you know that a song can be the catalyst for an awesome loving experience.

Music is one of the strongest tools we have to reconnect ourselves to our inner spirit. I hope you've had this kind of musical encounter at some point in your life. But even if you haven't, it's never too late to welcome a musical intervention. If you've felt frustrated, angry, or uninspired about certain areas of your life, you can use music to rejuvenate yourself from the inside out.

Do you want to shake a negative pattern? Make a positive-perception playlist. Create a mix of songs that spark your spirit and put a smile on your face. Listen to the playlist when you wake up in the morning, during your commute, at the gym, while you cook dinner, etc. Most important, use this playlist to shift your energy whenever you feel down. You can pack it with songs that are peaceful and calming or upbeat and energizing (or both). Let the music be your guide to reactivating your positive perceptions. Need a kick-start? Listen to my positive-perception playlists at Gabbyb.tv/Miracles-Now.

Use these playlists throughout the day. Far too often, we get bogged down with our busy schedules and to-do lists and forget to put on music and let our minds recalibrate. Schedule a few minutes a day to sit in stillness and listen to an inspiring song or two. Soften your mind as you let the music wash over you. This ritual will begin a powerful meditative practice of turning inward and releasing worldly concerns. In this stillness you can access your inspiration.

Today's Miracle Message is an opportunity for you to share your positive-perception playlist. You can simply post your own Spotify playlist or share one from this book. Here's a sample: Gabbyb.tv/Miracles-Now

Miracle Message #8:

Rev up your good vibes with my Positive-Perception Playlist! Gabbyb.tv/Miracles-Now

#MiraclesNow

#9: "WHEN YOU'RE FEELING HELPLESS, HELP SOMEONE."

Many people who come to my work feel a disconnection from their life's purpose. The issue isn't that they have no purpose; rather, it's that they forgot their true purpose. This principle will help you reclaim your true purpose: to be love and share love. This is the job of the miracle worker. *A Course in Miracles* teaches: "Miracles occur naturally as expressions of love. They are performed by those who temporarily have more for those who temporarily have less." As you open up to your inner power, it is important to accept that your life's true purpose is to be helpful to all.

Today, I'm introducing a powerful technique: regularly reciting a prayer from *A Course in Miracles*:

I am here only to be truly helpful.

I am here to represent Him who sent me.

I do not have to worry about what to say or what

to do, because He who sent me will direct me.

I am content to be wherever He wishes, knowing

He goes there with me.

I will be healed as I let Him teach me to heal.

The words of this prayer hold the energy and surrender of service. Once again you'll be guided to get out of your own way through serving others. As Nobel Peace Prize winner Auyn San Su Ki said, "When you're feeling helpless, help someone." Let your desire to be of service guide you to find your purpose.

For today's Miracle Message I suggest simply sharing the incredible Auyn San Su Ki quote. This message carries an energy that needs to be shared.

Miracle Message #9:

"When you're feeling helpless,
help someone." — Auyn San Su Ki

#MiraclesNow

#10: SLEEP IS A SPIRITUAL PRACTICE.

Restful sleep is a key ingredient to living a miraculous life. I'm not saying we need eight or ten hours a night to feel fully rested. In fact, sometimes less sleep can be more restorative than many hours. The key is to have real sleep . . . the drooling-on-the-pillow kind of sleep.

In an interview with Huffington Post President and Editor-in-Chief Arianna Huffington, she talked about how sleep is crucial to innovation. Huffington said, "The world is in desperate need of big ideas and there are many, many of them locked inside of us. We just need to close our eyes to see them. So, ladies and gentlemen, shut down your engines and get some sleep."

Huffington is right. Lack of sleep is another way we block our power, creativity, and intuition. We often measure our productivity based on how hard we work and how little we sleep. This mentality is negatively affecting our health and overall well-being. Throughout this book I'll emphasize the topic of how sleep is a spiritual practice. The first step is to accept that restorative rest begins with how we fall asleep.

I'm a hyper lady and often I've struggled to fall asleep. I believe that the way to get a restful night is to fall asleep properly. If you have trouble falling asleep or staying asleep through the night, use this Kundalini breathing technique to drift off and snooze soundly.

Step 1: Sit up straight in your bed.

Step 2: Breathe in using a U breath: Pucker your mouth as if you were holding a quarter between your lips. Breathe in.

Step 3: Exhale through your nose.

Continue this cycle of breath for one minute. Breathe in a U breath through your mouth and exhale through your nose. You will quickly feel rested. Then sleep tight!

Miracle Message #10:

Sleep is a spiritual practice.

#MiraclesNow

#11: WORRY IS A PRAYER FOR CHAOS.

Worry is a prayer for chaos. Unfortunately worrying can become a bad habit that takes over your thoughts and your life. Often people worry to avoid dealing with how they truly feel. This technique is about turning your worry upside down. Once again, become the nonjudgmental witness of your fear and begin to recognize when worry has the best of you. In the moment when you recognize your mind worrying, use this technique.

Simply stare at the tip of your nose.

Yup, that's right: Look down at the tip of your nose. This simple action can shut your mind off. It's a radical tool for disengaging worry and centering into a still mind. In any moment when worry begins to take you down, redirect by staring at the tip of your nose.

Today's Miracle Message will be very well received. So many people worry and obsess over every little issue. By simply sharing this message you can help people get out of their own way and release their need to worry.

Miracle Message #11:

Worry is a prayer for chaos.

#MiraclesNow

#12: "ALL MINDS ARE JOINED."

You know those groovy moments when you're thinking of someone and they call? These moments are not just wild coincidences. In fact, they're quite the opposite. These moments are reminders that we're all connected. What we think, we feel, and what we feel, we attract toward us. This concept greatly applies to our connection to other people.

Our logical mind convinces us that there is no divine order in how we connect to others. Whereas *A Course in Miracles* says, "There are no accidents in salvation. Those who are to meet will meet, because together they have the potential for a holy relationship. They are ready for each other." Taking this point into consideration, use this message to begin to bust through any boundaries you experience with others. Maybe you feel disconnected from a lover, or maybe you can't understand why it seems your boss doesn't like you. These conflicts can lead you to act in certain ways to make yourself heard or put up a wall of protection so you don't get hurt. Today's practice will help you establish a connection with any person, no matter how difficult or distant that relationship may feel.

The *Course* teaches, "All minds are joined." Today's technique will give you tools to use in your day-to-day life so you can recognize and accept the great truth from Yogi Bhajan: "The other person is you." Use this meditation to accept and remember that we're all in this together; we are all one.

Sit comfortably in a chair or on the floor.

Begin breathing in your nose and out your nose.

Take long, deep breaths.

As you continue to breathe, hold a vision in your mind of the person whom you've had conflict with.

Envision them standing before you.

As you breathe in, envision white light pouring into your heart.

As you exhale, extend this light to their heart.

Continue this cycle of breath.

Allow this exchange of light to melt away your resentment and restore you to a sense of oneness.

The awesome thing about this meditation is that you can do it anywhere. You can be sitting across the room from someone in an office and envision yourself sending them light. Or you can be many miles away and have the same energetic effect. Don't be surprised if the person calls or sends you some kind of loving message when you're done with the meditation. But don't meditate for outcomes—meditate for peace.

Once again, it's time to carry the message. Use today's Miracle Message to remind your friends and family that we're all connected.

Miracle Message #12:

"All minds are joined." — *A Course in Miracles*

#ACIM #MiraclesNow

#13: WHERE IS THE LOVE?

When we feel stuck it's because we choose to perceive our situation with fear rather than love. Wherever there is love, there is a way to get unstuck. All boundaries rise up because we forget to call on love.

This exercise will remind you that you can dissolve all boundaries with love. *A Course in Miracles* teaches us, "The only thing that can be lacking in any situation is that which you are not giving." This is a really empowering message: It reminds us that we're in charge of our own lives and that we don't have to wait for some external force to change our circumstances. So if you're feeling stuck in a situation or caught up in a negative pattern, ask yourself, "Where is the love?" Simply asking this question can catapult you into a new perspective. Take a moment to review the situation and identify where love is missing. Then make a mental note of all the ways you can be more kind, giving, and loving toward yourself, other people, and your perception of the situation.

For instance, if you're feeling stuck in a relationship and blaming yourself or the other person for the blocks, simply say, "Where is the love?" Search your mind for all the loving thoughts, outcomes, or circumstances that can replace the fear you've chosen to perceive. Make a mental list (or a written list) of new ways to experience the situation, and choose one to commit to. Maybe you choose to focus on what you love about the person rather than all the little things that piss you off. Or maybe in the moment when you catch yourself attacking them you choose to re-interpret the situation with a more loving attitude. Commit to your new perception and let it become your reality. Accept that in any given moment you can dissolve all boundaries with love.

Miracle Message #13:
Dissolve all boundaries with love.
#MiraclesNow

#14: SNAP OUT OF IT!

One of the primary reasons for our unhappiness and discomfort is our attack thoughts. All day long, without even realizing it, we're attacking ourselves and others. Attacks don't have to be massive to inflict real damage—each small attack, from a negative thought about ourselves to a cold comment toward another person, adds up. Attack breeds attack. Attacking others in our mind or in our actions directly harms us.

Our attack thoughts and actions are particularly dangerous because they can be so subtle and insidious that we might not realize how much they've taken over our minds. But as fiendish as they are, they're surprisingly easy to let go of. All it takes is an ordinary rubber band.

One day—today—wear a rubber band on your wrist. Whenever you notice an attack thought arise, flick your rubber band against your arm. Does this seem jarring? Good! It's exactly what you need to literally snap yourself out of your unconscious attack thoughts.

Once you've snapped out of the attack cycle, it's time to clean up your thoughts. Use this exercise based on lesson 23 of *A Course in Miracles*: "I can escape from the world I see by giving up attack thoughts."

The moment you snap the rubber band, witness your attack thought and say to yourself: *I can escape from the world I see by giving up attack thoughts about* _____ . You can fill in the blank with whatever you're attacking, whether it's broad or very specific.

Practice this exercise throughout the day. Notice your attack thought, snap out of it with your rubber band, and then use the *Course* message as a reminder that you can think your way out in an instant.

Miracle Message #14:

"I can escape from the world I see by giving up attack thoughts."

#ACIM #MiraclesNow

#15: BUST THROUGH
THE BLOCKS WITH
BREATH OF FIRE.

One of the greatest ways to bust through emotional blocks fast is with a breathing technique frequently used in Kundalini yoga. It's called "breath of fire." Breath of fire is a rhythmic breath in and out the nose, kind of like deep sniffing. On the inhale, your diaphragm extends; on the exhale, it releases. Once you get into a rhythm, you speed up the breath until it becomes breath of fire.

Breath of fire newbies often put emphasis on the exhale. This is a common mistake that can be easily corrected by remembering that the inhale and exhale are even. It is also common for the newcomer to experience shortness of breath. This means that your diaphragm is tight from stress and tension or that you're breathing in the opposite direction. Remember that on the inhale your diaphragm extends, while on the exhale it contracts. Through your deep breaths do your best to keep your diaphragm re-laxed. As you practice breath of fire you will release the tension in your diaphragm and in effect release yourself from many emotional blocks.

Breath of fire has many benefits beyond busting through the blocks. It purifies and oxygenates your blood-stream, increases your body's energy flow, stimulates the pituitary gland (which helps bring all the other glands into balance), and strengthens your electromagnetic field so you become a magnet for greatness. One minute of breath of fire can bring about the same benefits you'd experience in one hour holding the same pose with a normal breath.

Miracle Message #15:

When you feel blocked, emotionally distressed, or overwhelmed, turn to your breath.

#MiraclesNow

#16: MAKE FORGIVENESS
A PRACTICE.

In all my books, lectures, and teachings I emphasize the importance of practicing the F-word like a full-time job. The experience of forgiveness is rooted in all spiritual teachings and is the method through which we release the past and reclaim love in the present. Forgiveness is a great way to become unstuck and open up to a more vibrant life.

When you're unforgiving, you feel stuck, weak, angry, and resentful. All those feelings contain low-level energy and therefore block your capacity to heal, grow, and live life to the fullest.

Forgiveness offers you a way out. Through forgiveness you can learn to let go of littleness and crack open to your true inner light. Like many things, forgiveness is a habit. Get into it by learning to forgive yourself first.

Yogi Bhajan once said to a room full of his students, "The only difference between me and you is that I practice forgiving myself all day long." Yogi Bhajan shows us that a key to being the master of your own mind is to learn how to forgive yourself. So for today, just for one minute, practice forgiving yourself. Make it a conscious, purposeful action. It only takes a few moments, but it's radically transformational.

The moment you recognize your self-attack, follow these four steps:

1. Witness the attack thought.

2. Breathe into the feeling of discomfort.

3. Feel the feeling.

4. Say to yourself, "I forgive this thought. I know it is not real."

Practice these four steps and prepare yourself to go deeper into the forgiveness process. In technique #83, you'll be guided to heighten your forgiveness and experience true freedom.

Miracle Message #16:

"Forgiveness is not an occasional act, it is a constant attitude." — Dr. Martin Luther King, Jr.

#MiraclesNow

#17: MEDITATE TO RELEASE CHILDHOOD ANGER.

So much of what holds us back in life are the long-held resentments stemming from childhood. In our youth we create many of the stories that we play out as adults—stories of unworthiness, self-hatred, victimhood, and many more. As young children we learned about separation and specialness. We were taught to see ourselves as less than or better than others. We learned inequality. That separation made us angry, and we carried the anger into our adulthood.

Our childhood anger is a huge part of our neuroses and unhappiness. If we are to move forward in life, we must move through our anger to access our true energy source. This meditation will help you release childhood anger so that you can truly tune in to your own subtle powers.

Meditation for Releasing Childhood Anger

Sit in Easy Pose with your arms stretched out straight to the sides. There is no bend in the elbows. Use your thumbs to lock down the Mercury and Sun fingers (pinkie and ring fingers) and extend the Jupiter and Saturn fingers (index and middle fingers). The palms face forward and the fingers point out to the sides (as seen in the pictures).

The breath is unique in that you inhale by sucking air through your closed teeth and exhale through your nose. It is suggested that you practice this meditation for 11 minutes, though you can start with 1 minute and build up.

To finish the meditation, inhale deeply and hold your breath for ten seconds while you stretch your spine up and your arms out to the sides. Then exhale. Repeat this two more times.

If you feel stuck in or held back by childhood anger, use this meditation regularly or begin a 40-day practice. The meditation will change you inside and out. You can practice it in the morning and the evening. Yogi Bhajan said that if you practice the meditation in the evening, when you wake up your whole energy will have changed.

Miracle Message #17:

Releasing anger from the past
sets me free in the present.

#MiraclesNow

#18: JUST ASK!

Do you ever get angry and resentful because you're not getting what you want? Or do you feel your needs are not being met? If you do feel like this, then I have another question for you: Do you ask for what you want?

When you feel you're not getting what you want from others, the easiest thing to do is complain about it. But blaming other people for your feelings of dissatisfaction is the wrong way to approach the issue. The key to getting what you want is to ASK FOR IT.

Asking can be really uncomfortable for some folks. I see this often when it comes to asking for a raise, asking for help, or merely asking someone to listen to what you have to say. As difficult as it can be to ask, it's important to realize that you won't get what you want until you're willing to put it out there.

If you tend to freak out about asking for what you want, it's time to shake off the fear and change your ways. What you'll come to learn is that, deep down, all people genuinely want to give. Therefore, when you ask for something from a place of authenticity and grace, your request will be met with mutual respect. Now's the time to create a new habit and get your asking muscles in motion!

Begin the process of asking for what you want by following these three steps.

Step 1: Accept that it may feel uncomfortable and awkward at first. You've likely spent most of your life unwilling to ask for what you want—so testing out new behavior will feel strange. Remember that the strangeness is a good sign. Regardless of how uncomfortable you feel, take this powerful action in the right direction and step outside your comfort zone.

Step 2: Get clear about what you're asking for. Make sure you're clear about what you want. When you're clear about what you're asking for, your energy is committed to the request. But if you're unclear, your energy wavers, which makes it more difficult to really get behind your request. It's also really important to back up your request with positive intentions. When your request is backed with the energy of love, it will be received with love.

Step 3: Just ask! The moment you notice yourself avoiding the chance to ask for what you want, move swiftly past your fear and just ask. Though you may be scared, this simple yet courageous act of asking can change your life in an instant. You'll come to know a new sense of self-respect that will give others the freedom to respect you back.

Stop playing small: Speak up, own your power, and ask for what you want.

Miracle Message #18:
The key to getting what you want is to ASK FOR IT.
#MiraclesNow

#19: BE MORE CHILDLIKE.

It's easy to get caught up in the to-do lists and daily tasks. When there are bills to pay and people to support, happiness can become a distant afterthought. When our energy is focused only on getting things done, we can lose sight of what makes us happy.

We often make the mistake of thinking that we'll be most productive, satisfied, and happy by focusing our energy on our daily tasks and commitments. We blast through our to-do lists with the idea that we can relax and enjoy life once the last item has been crossed off. The truth is that there will always be another to-do. There will always be another task. If we're constantly focused only on our responsibilities, we sap our own energy and cut off our life-flow.

It may seem counterintuitive, but one key to feeling more productive and satisfied is to step away from your responsibilities from time to time. Whenever you feel caught up in a do-do-do mind-set, close your laptop, turn off your phone, and tap into your childlike self. Children have an enormous capacity for curiosity, creativity, and openness.

Let go of the pressure you've put on yourself and unleash your inner child with these few tips.

Be more curious: An incredible way to get out of your head is to get curious about something new. One of the coolest things about kids is that they're super curious. Like a kid, spend time throughout your day being curious about new things. Read a magazine you'd never typically pick up, ask more questions, and try a new kind of food. Curiosity will take you out of whatever it was you were obsessing over and lead you into a state of simple innocence.

Be more present: Becoming more present in every moment will help you release the pressure you put on yourself. Children are awesome at wholeheartedly experiencing the moment. Act like an innocent child. Taste your food with more wonder, notice the colors of the sky, and laugh louder than you normally do.

Daydream: Rather than occupy your mind with chaotic thoughts, take a dream break. Sit on a park bench and daydream. Spend five to ten minutes thinking your way into a cool experience you'd always hoped to have. This process will not only get you out of your own way but it will help you make your dreams become your reality.

Practice any one of these tools and you'll feel yourself becoming unstuck as your creative energy flows more freely. When you step back from your to-do list to let your freewheeling inner kid come forth, you can go back to your grown-up responsibilities with a fresh perspective and renewed energy.

Miracle Message #19:

To relinquish control, simply
let loose and be more childlike.

#MiraclesNow

#20: INTENTIONS GROW WHEN THEY'RE SHARED.

Life can throw all kinds of obstacles and traumas our way. Experiences such as family or personal illness, job loss, and even tragedies in the news can make us feel powerless. In these moments we have a choice: we can internalize our experience and isolate, or we can turn to others for help.

One way to soothe yourself and find power in powerless situations is to gather with groups of like-minded people. Group prayer, intention setting, and meditation can offer you and the world tremendous healing.

Connecting to group energy is an amazing way to instantly relieve the acute pain of emotional trauma. A great example of group recovery is the twelve-step method. One reason the twelve-step program has had so much success is that people come together for shared healing and harmonious connections. The supportive energy of the group fortifies each person's positive intentions and gives everyone a safe outlet for dealing with trauma and difficulty. Often in twelve-step communities, people suggest that God can be the group of people who wrap around you during your recovery. God is in the group and through the group you find God.

There are several ways to connect with others when you're feeling helpless. Of course, not everyone winds up in a twelve-step meeting or a recovery group—but there are great ways you can establish group connection instantly.

If you don't have people in your community ready to hop on the love train, then join a group online. If you're a woman reading this, check out my site HerFuture.com, a digital sisterhood. If you're a man reading this, join me on my Facebook fan page (Facebook.com/GabrielleBernstein) where you can connect to like-minded miracle workers and me! I encourage you not only to ask for help but also to offer your help to those in need. By simply visiting this page for one minute a day, you will feel the collective group community.

If there are people in your life who have your back, don't hesitate to reach out for help. We forget so easily that when we ask others to help us we're helping them, too. Giving someone the chance to serve opens their heart and changes their attitude. So reach out and call someone. Get on the phone with a friend or two and ask them to join you in setting a positive intention for your situation. *A Course in Miracles* says, "When two or more join together in searching for truth, the ego can no longer defend its lack of content. The fact of union tells them it is not true."

The *Course* reminds us that when we join together seeking truth, we can remind each other of what is real.

Remember that allowing others to support you supports them in turn. When you feel powerless and alone, use these exercises to find power in positive group energy.

Miracle Message #20:

When you allow others to support you, you support them, too.

#MiraclesNow

#21: MEDIDATE FOR A DATE.

I can't tell you how often I hear people complain about dating—whether in my group coaching classes or in everyday conversations, struggles with dating come up over and over again. It is my firm belief that there are three main blocks keeping people from joyful dating.

The first block is that many people carry their disastrous past dates into the present moment. Maybe the last guy you went out with never called you back, and you're still angry about it. Holding on to that anger only smothers your next date with negative vibes, even if you plaster a smile on your face all evening. This anger keeps you rooted in your history and robs you of the opportunity to fully experience the now.

The second block is a lack of clarity. Unfocused desires bring unfocused results. If you don't clarify what you want out of a date, you will continue to attract people who are wrong for you.

The final issue blocking folks from great dates is the achieve-achieve-achieve mentality. Just because you can make things happen in other areas of your life doesn't mean you can control your dating life, too. You might be a super productive go-getter at work, but it simply doesn't translate to the dating world. Leave your "get after it" mentality behind and relax into the dating process.

So—how can you overcome these dating hurdles?

The answer is MediDating!

Now that you've identified the blocks, it's time to bring in the tool to release those blocks. MediDating is a method I created that uses the practice of meditation to release fears, raise your confidence, and unleash your attracting power. To help you in the MediDating process, I've included three guided meditations that you can access for free at Gabbyb.tv/MediDate.

Releasing romantic illusions meditation

This guided meditation is perfect if you feel stuck in a rut. If you're carrying past resentments toward former lovers, this one's for you! Use this meditation to help you clear the fears, anger, and doubts that have been holding you back from experiencing love. Listen at Gabbyb.tv/MediDate.

Pre-date meditation

This meditation is the one to practice before you leave for a date. The key to successful dating is to show up with your authentic self. There is nothing sexier than your truth. Use this meditation to release your pre-date jitters and center into your authenticity. Bring YOU to the date and it will be a massive success. Listen at Gabbyb.tv/MediDate.

Manifesting meditation

This meditation is sacred. It will help you tap into how you want to feel in a romantic relationship. The way to truly manifest your desires is to focus on how you want to feel — that feeling is what attracts love to you. When you practice this meditation, be prepared to tap into your love zone and get ready for romance! Listen at Gabbyb.tv/MediDate.

Release your dating illusions and start Medi-Dating today!

Miracle Message #21:

I am ready to receive love.

#MiraclesNow

#22: LOSE THE STAGE FRIGHT.

Whether it's having to give a keynote address, a presentation at work, or even a wedding toast, we can count on being in the spotlight at some point. Regardless of the size of the group, it can be intimidating to speak publicly. For some people, speaking publicly can be completely paralyzing. I've witnessed perfectly confident people clam up the moment they have to. The debilitating experience of stage fright can be a major block in moving forward in a career, or even sharing your talents.

Stage fright comes from limiting beliefs such as, "It's not safe to speak publicly" or "I won't be accepted for what I have to say." If you want to change this age-old phobia, you have to tinker with part of the brain that triggers stage fright (and all other fears): the amygdala. The amygdala plays a major role in storing memories associated with emotional events. When it's triggered, it has the capacity to hijack the logical brain and lead us into fight-or-flight mode.

Applying pressure on certain meridians of the body can modulate your amygdala and release you from the illusion that you're unsafe. The simple act of pressing down on a certain body meridian (a meridian is a Chinese medicine principle that there is a path through which life-energy flows) can establish a new emotion that helps you calm down and create a new experience.

This tool is similar to the Emotional Freedom Technique (EFT), otherwise known as tapping. The concept is that when we tap on certain energy meridians, we can unblock stagnant emotions and trigger a new experience in the brain. (Learn more about tapping in technique #25.)

My dear friend and Kundalini teacher Joseph Amanbir Young, who is also a licensed acupuncturist, focuses on helping people release stress and tension, and create new emotional patterns. He says, "Each meridian point has a different influence on our psyche. For stage fright a simple tool is to apply pressure to a point on the back of the forearm. This point's name is 'Outer Pass' and allows us to pass through situations where we need to be 'out' to the world with courage and self-reliance."

Gripped by stage fright? Amanbir says to apply medium pressure to the back of your forearm (either arm works!) approximately three inches from the back of the wrist. Hold the pressure for one to three minutes.

This one-minute miracle can help you release stage fright and guide you to establish a new emotional pattern. Use this tool whenever you need to speak publicly—and remember, the world needs you to share your light!

Miracle Message #22:

I speak with confidence because
the world needs my light.

#MiraclesNow

#23: PRAY BEFORE YOU PAY.

I have to admit that I used to be one of those people who let the bills pile up. Yup, I was that girl. Every month the stack on my desk grew bigger and wobblier. Each time I looked at it, I felt pangs of frustration over having to pay them. Maybe it stemmed from an old fear of not having enough, or maybe I was just exercising my self-sabotage muscles. Whatever the issue, it was a pretty awful monthly ritual.

Then it became clear to me that my bad habit was blocking me in many ways and creating unnecessary frustration and guilt. My bill pile was cluttering up my desk space—a real no-no. The ancient Chinese method of feng shui emphasizes releasing all clutter in the office space. Clutter has a profound impact on our emotional, mental, physical, and spiritual well-being. The value of clearing the clutter is that it releases vital energy that helps with mental clarity, inspiration, and even our earning capacity!

So my first step toward healing my relationship with my bills was to clear the clutter off my desk. I gathered my pile of bills and organized each statement in a beautiful green box. (If your bills are all paperless, you can make a similar move with your e-mail. Simply create colored labels or folders for each bill and organize them as they come in, so you're never searching for the latest e-mail statement.)

Once I was organized, I committed to bringing my spiritual practice to my monthly bills. I sat with my beautiful green box and prayed over each bill before cutting a check. I said, "Thank you, Universe, for providing me with the resources to pay these bills. I am grateful to contribute to the economy and to support my growing business." Simply saying this prayer before paying each bill energized me. I was infused with an attitude of gratitude rather than an essence of anxiety and tension.

Now my bill-paying process is much more enjoyable and my desk is clutter-free. To top it all off, as soon as I cleared my desk space I started to notice many more new career opportunities come through. Money began to flow more freely once I cleared the space to receive it.

If you're someone who experiences a lot of anxiety around paying bills, use these tips to bust through the block. Clear your desk and pray before you pay!

Miracle Message #23:

Pray before you pay.

#MiraclesNow

#24: COMPARE NO MORE.

Comparing is a nasty habit. When we compare ourselves to others we get hooked into the belief that we're
better than or less than someone else. Comparing creates
animosity, resentment, jealousy, and competition. Living
in this way can hurt your happiness and your sense of
peace. How can you be peaceful when you're constantly
comparing yourself? It's exhausting!

Beneath the desire to compare is a deep-rooted sense
that we are not enough. When we feel an unconscious
sense of lack, we project that lack onto others so we won't
feel so bad about ourselves. It's a vicious cycle. For instance, maybe you've been single for a while and you often
compare yourself to people who are in relationships. This
act of comparing sends you into a tizzy, reinforcing all
that you don't have and convincing you that attached folks
are better than you. Or maybe you compare yourself to
celebrities and notable figures. You always see yourself as
less than and in effect you feel incomplete. Understanding this pattern is the first step toward transforming it.

Once you're aware of your comparing habit, the next
step is to take action toward changing your behavior. The
moment you witness yourself comparing, pause and say
(whether out loud or to yourself): "The light I see in them
is a reflection of my inner light." Even if you don't believe
this affirmation or you think it's too New Agey, give it a
shot. Each time you compare, recite the affirmation.

Choosing to perceive oneness in the moment can release you from the need to compare. In an instant, you can be set free. That is a miracle.

Practice this tool as often as possible and pay attention to your shifts. The shifts may be subtle at first, but you'll feel relief right away. Set yourself free from the comparison cycle and be at peace with who you are.

Miracle Message #24:

Whenever you compare yourself to others,
simply say this prayer: "The light I see in them is a
reflection of my inner light."

#MiraclesNow

#25: TAP THAT STRESS!

Stress has become an epidemic. When was the last time you said, "I'm so stressed out"? This week? Today? I hear it all the time—for lots of people, it seems to be their default state. In many cases, stress stems from unhealed past experiences that have created fear-based beliefs in the present. We become stressed whenever memories of those experiences are triggered. For instance, maybe you were told you were overweight as a child. Now, whenever it's mealtime, you're triggered by the food on the table, which causes stress and fear around eating. Or maybe you have an old limiting belief that you're not a good reader. Then whenever you're asked to read out loud, stress arises and you feel overwhelmed with fear.

Here's how it works: We encounter a trigger, at which point cortisol (the stress hormone) is secreted into the bloodstream. While cortisol is important to the body's response to stress, it's also important that we experience a relaxation period or we can't return to a normal state. Our rushed, high-stress lifestyles usually don't equip us with the tools to return to relaxation. That's how stress becomes chronic—we have consistently high levels of cortisol in our bloodstream. These high levels of cortisol can have major negative effects on the body. Extreme stress can lead to a blood sugar imbalance, poor concentration, high blood pressure, thyroid dysfunction, and many more negative symptoms. The good news is that a stress-free life is available to us all. We just need the necessary tools for releasing stress on a moment-to-moment basis.

For stress management, I routinely practice EFT: the Emotional Freedom Technique, otherwise known as tapping. EFT is a psychological acupressure technique that supports your emotional health. I have found that tapping is one of the greatest ways to bust through the blocks in an instant. Throughout the book, expect to see more tapping exercises to support specific blocks. (If you want a tapping deep-dive, check out my friend Nick Ortner's incredible book, *The Tapping Solution*.)

This exercise will be a great way to bring tapping into your life. You can tap on any issue that arises, whether you're stressed about work, feeling pressure in your personal life, or anything else. This tool requires that you tap on specific points that align with your body's energy meridians. Each meridian specified in tapping relates to a specific organ or body part. When you stimulate these meridians, you tell the amygdala (the fight-or-flight part of the brain) to calm down. When the amygdala gets the memo that it's safe to relax, stress is immediately reduced. As you tap on the specific points, you'll be guided through my script to address certain emotions that come up around your stress. Simply follow my script and use the visual guide to learn the location of each tapping point. Let the tapping begin!

Whenever you begin a tapping session, you start with the Most Pressing Issue, or MPI. In this case, the MPI is related to stress. Let's use the phrase, *I'm stressed out and overwhelmed.* Before we begin, rate this MPI on a scale of 1 to 10, 10 being the most painful.

Use the script that follows and tap on the specified areas of your body as you say the suggested phrases. Before you begin, review each tapping point in the image below.

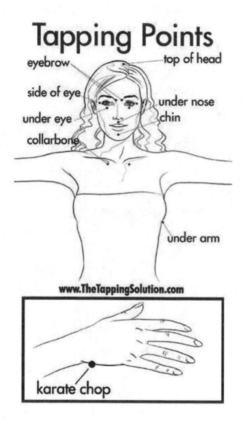

Start by tapping on the karate chop point. Tap lightly on each point approximately seven times. As you tap, repeat the following phrase three times: *Even though I'm stressed out and overwhelmed, I deeply and completely accept myself.*

Karate chop: *Even though I'm stressed out and overwhelmed, I deeply and completely accept myself.*

Karate chop: *Even though I'm stressed out and overwhelmed, I deeply and completely accept myself.*

Karate chop: *Even though I'm stressed out and overwhelmed, I deeply and completely accept myself.*

Continue tapping on the other points and say each of these out loud as you do:

Eyebrow: *All this stress is freaking me out.*

Side of eye: *I feel overwhelmed and scared.*

Under eye: *I don't think I can accomplish everything.*

Under nose: *If I don't accomplish everything, I'll be even more stressed out.*

Chin: *All this stress is overwhelming me.*

Collarbone: *I'm afraid that I won't get it all done.*

Under arm: *This fear is causing more stress.*

Top of head: *I just can't calm down.*

Eyebrow: *I can't imagine how I'll accomplish everything.*

Side of eye: *All this stress.*

Under eye: *All this fear is rising.*

Under nose: *It's hard to breathe when I'm stressed.*

Chin: *I can't manage my life without getting stressed.*

Collarbone: *I'm afraid to let go of control.*

Under arm: *I must stay in control.*

Top of head: *I'm scared of my stress.*

Continue to tap through the "negative rounds" (all the statements about how stressed you are) until you begin to feel a sense of relief. The moment you feel a sense of relief, begin tapping through the "positive round," and say each phrase below out loud.

Eyebrow: *I know this stress isn't serving me.*

Side of eye: *I believe I can live stress-free.*

Under eye: *My true accomplishments will come through ease.*

Under nose: *When I'm calm, I'll have more energy to get everything done.*

Chin: *I no longer need this stress.*

Collarbone: *I am ready to release this overwhelm.*

Under arm: *I can relax now.*

Top of head: *I am calm now.*

Tap through the positive statements as many times as you'd like until you feel genuine relief.

When you're done, say your MPI out loud: *Even though I'm stressed out and overwhelmed, I deeply and completely accept myself.* Now rate it from 1 to 10 and compare it to when you first began.

If you tapped through each round with commitment, you're sure to have experienced relief. In some cases you may drop from a 10 to 2 in just a minute of tapping. This tool is one of the most powerful ways to bust through blocks in an instant. If you didn't feel relief, don't worry! Just keep tapping. It may take a little getting used to, but your mind and body will respond. Tap on!

Miracle Message #25:

Ancient pain *can* be released simply by feeling it.

#MiraclesNow

#26: THINK YOUR WAY OUT.

Without even realizing it, we can think our way into a tizzy. One thought leads to the next until they're tumbling into one another and you're hooked into a fearful delusion. For instance, maybe you've been obsessing about losing your job. The moment your boss shows up in a bad mood your fear kicks in and your thoughts go wild. You think your way into the worst-case scenario, envisioning the moment your boss calls you into his office to fire you. Then you think your way into the moment you leave the office with your stuff packed into a filing box. Next, you think about how hard it will be to pay the bills and all the responsibilities you have. Now you're gripped by terror, on the verge of a panic attack at your desk, and the next half-hour is shot. Yet all this chaos was created in your mind based on one tiny mad idea about your job. Meanwhile, your boss showed up in a bad mood because of his own issue, not yours! This is a clear example of how most of the anxiety we experience is based on fearful thoughts rather than reality.

Psychologists have estimated that we have more than 60,000 thoughts a day, and 95 to 99 percent of those thoughts are repeated. It's likely that you are far too familiar with your repetitive thoughts, such as, *I don't have enough, That will never work out*, or *I'm not good enough for that partner* . . . and so on.

The key to redirecting the pattern of our thoughts is to proactively choose new ones. This exercise requires commitment and dedication, but man, is it worth it! Here's the gist: Every time you notice your thoughts spin toward crazy town, use the rubber band method from technique 14. Flick the rubber band to snap yourself out of the fear cycle. Then immediately think your way out. One thought at a time, reach for a higher, more loving perspective.

Let's use the job example again to illustrate. Same situation: your boss comes to work in a bad mood and your fear of getting fired is triggered. Instead of going down the fear spiral, you snap your rubber band to redirect your thoughts. Then right away you reach for a positive perspective. Your next thoughts can be: *I know that he's come to work in a bad mood, but it's probably his own stuff. I'm going to send positive thoughts to my boss so he can release what's pissing him off. I trust that my positive attitude and empowering approach to life will help me keep this job secure. I know I am a great worker and that people love to be around me. I feel confident in my skills and I trust in my credentials. My job is secure. I am at peace. All is well.*

As you can see, this is a much more positive way to handle your thoughts. The simple act of thinking your way out of fear can change your entire experience. As you raise your thoughts, you raise your energy and therefore become a match for more desirable experiences. Trust in the power of your thoughts and take them very seriously. In just one minute you can think your way out of fear and back to love. Practice this principle whenever you catch fear sneaking in.

Miracle Message #26:

I can think my way out of fear.

#MiraclesNow

#27: FORGIVE AND DELETE.

One day I got a frantic call from my mother. She breathlessly told me: "There's someone on your Facebook fan page writing nasty things about you! But don't worry, honey, I responded and set her straight." I laughed and said, "Thanks for sticking up for me, Mom, but that's not how I handle negativity on the Internet." I went on to explain that, as a spiritual student and teacher, I must practice what I preach. I helped my mother understand that engaging in the negativity only invests in the negativity. Rather than defend myself and fight back, I've learned to see these encounters as divine spiritual assignments. Through compassion, defenselessness, and forgiveness, I've come to see how mindfully dealing with Internet haters can only strengthen my spiritual faith.

As the universe would have it, that wouldn't be my only conversation about Internet haters that week. The following day, I was in Chicago shooting a segment for Oprah's show, *Super Soul Sunday*. What was one of Oprah's first questions to my panel? She asked how we handle haters on the Internet! I immediately responded, "Forgive and delete."

If you're anything like my mother, it's time to put down the boxing gloves and use this principle for handling haters.

Have compassion for these folks. Let's face it: Happy people don't post rude comments on the Web. Compassion will reconnect you to a sense of oneness and defenselessness, which will help you put down the boxing gloves and settle into a new perspective. Just let go fully and forgive. To really seal the deal, I suggest you use prayer. Simply say, "I pray to forgive you and release you." Then feel free to block or delete the user or hide the comment. If you have the power to clear the feed, let that become part of your practice. There's no reason to let negative comments linger. Simply forgive and delete.

Miracle Message #27:

How to handle haters on the Internet? Forgive and delete!

#MiraclesNow

#28: DISH OUT COMPLIMENTS SINCERELY AND LIBERALLY.

As great as it feels to get compliments, it's equally impactful to give them. Offering love and kindness can, in an instant, shift your energy and support your nervous system. Many scientific journals suggest that there is a strong link between compassion and the vagus nerve, which regulates the heart and controls inflammation levels in the body. Vagus is Latin for "wandering," which is apt—this long nerve roams all through the body and has a lot of influence. One study focused on the loving-kindness meditation, a staple in Tibetan Buddhism. The researchers found that kindness and compassion reduced inflammation in the body due to their effect on the vagus nerve.

Along with the health benefits of kindness come emotional benefits. When we offer up love and kindness to others, we center into our natural state. *A Course in Miracles* teaches, "Kindness created me kind." This message reminds us that our true nature is to be kind and loving toward all. Unfortunately, we lose sight of our true kindness when the fear-based ways of the world set in. Therefore, the more we practice random acts of kindness the better we feel because we are exercising our truth.

One of the greatest ways to share love and kindness is to compliment someone. This is simple. Take time out of your day to pay someone a genuine compliment. It doesn't matter whether you know the person (in fact, complimenting a stranger is a great way to create an instant positive connection). Just dish out the compliment sincerely. Make sure to pay attention to the way the energy shifts in the other person. Witness their inner light flicker on and let it illuminate your own mood. When you compliment another person, you're complimenting yourself. Kindness is a boomerang.

Miracle Message #28:

Dish out compliments sincerely and liberally.

#MiraclesNow

#29: YOU ARE NOT YOUR HABITS.

Throughout my life I've given up many bad habits. Most recently I stopped drinking coffee—and letting go of it was not easy. In fact, strange as it may sound, it was even harder than when I got sober and gave up drugs and alcohol. Caffeine was my last drug, and because it wasn't killing me I continued to give myself permission to drink it.

One of the main reasons we stay stuck in habits we know don't serve us is because of our permission-giving thoughts, such as, *One cup of coffee a day won't kill me.* Or, *I only drink on weekends.* These thoughts keep us convinced that there is nothing wrong with our behavior, even though deep down we know it isn't right.

In many cases we use our bad habits to avoid dealing with something much more difficult. In my case, I was using coffee as a final vice. As a sober woman I felt I deserved something I could turn to when I felt I needed a jolt. This habit seemed harmless, but when I got honest with myself, it became clear that I was just using the coffee as another drug. Upon genuinely reviewing my behavior, I came to realize that I had to stop giving myself permission to drink coffee and that it was time to change the habit.

Transitioning out of a bad habit can be really uncomfortable at first. To help you ease into the process, I've outlined the three steps that worked for me when I put down the coffee.

Step 1: Keep it in the day. One of the main reasons we get tripped up when we try to change a habit is that we start future-tripping. For instance, when I was first letting go of coffee, I'd project onto the future with thoughts such as, *What will I do when I'm in Europe and I want a cappuccino?* What helped me most during these future flip-outs was to simply keep it in the day. I would tell myself, *I don't need to worry about tomorrow. Today I choose not to drink coffee.* One day at a time I've stayed committed.

Step 2: Change your breath pattern. The moment we change our breath pattern, we change our energy, thereby changing our experience. Whenever you notice yourself about to relapse into your negative behavior, take a long, deep breath. As you change your breath, you change your energy. Your calm and centered energy will support you in positive behavior and stop you from indulging in your bad habit.

Step 3: Make it joyful. Letting go of a negative habit doesn't have to be torturous. In fact, it can be joyful. To create real change we need more than just willpower: We must find the joy and curiosity in our new circumstances. Letting go of a bad habit is really just creating a new habit. In that new habit, you can find happiness. In my case, I chose not to dwell on the loss of coffee and instead I fell in love with organic tea.

If you're ready to let go of a vice that's been plaguing you, use these three steps and find joy in creating new habits.

Miracle Message #29:

I can change my patterns
when I change my mind about them.
#MiraclesNow

#30: USE A BACKPACK
MEDITATION.

Throughout the day we encounter stress triggers. We can be triggered by all kinds of circumstances, people, noises—even the weather. Yogi Bhajan said that 85 percent of our behavior is automatic and determined by our environment. If we let our environment dictate our mood, then our life will feel like an emotional roller coaster. The only way off the roller coaster is through our breath.

You may consider breathing an afterthought and pay little attention to the rhythm and depth of your inhales and exhales. Maybe you've never learned how to breathe properly. When I introduce breath to a new audience, I'm amazed at how many people are breathing the *opposite* way that they should! The proper way to breathe is the yogic breath that expands the lungs and the diaphragm. This method of breath is simple: breathe in and your diaphragm expands, breathe out and it contracts. To make sure you're doing this correctly, place your hand on your stomach and make sure your stomach is extending on the inhale and contracting on the exhale.

Check in with yourself. Is this how you've been breathing? If not, then you've been strangling yourself. That's okay! Just change the pattern today.

Consciously turning to our breath for help is not our initial response to stress. Most of us are more likely to raise our voice, throw a fit, or burst into tears. Instead of losing your cool, use this exercise to bring you back to peace.

This is called the backpack meditation. You can store this meditation in your backpack and use it whenever and wherever stress arises. It will save you each time.

Here's how it works.

The posture: Sit cross-legged in Easy Pose.

The hands: Place your hands in your lap with your thumb pressing against your index finger. This is called the Gyan mudra. A mudra is a hand position that guides energy flow to the brain by connecting to specific energy meridians. When you press your thumb against this finger you ignite your knowledge. The index finger is symbolized by Jupiter, and the thumb represents the ego. Gyan mudra supports receptivity and calm.

GABRIELLE BERNSTEIN

The breath: This Kundalini meditation suggests that you breathe in eight breaths through your nose and breathe out one breath through your nose. (Visit the video on Gabbyb.tv/Miracles-Now for the visual explanation.) If yogic breath is new to you and it's hard to breathe in that much air, then breathe in for four breaths instead of eight. Breathe in four breaths through the nose, then exhale one breath.

Time: You can do this meditation for one minute and experience miraculous results. Put this meditation in your back pocket and use it whenever you feel stressed, frazzled, or tense. The Kundalini yogis suggest that you do this meditation for 11 minutes for 40 days. You can begin with 3 minutes and build up to 11.

Pay close attention to how your environment triggers your stress patterns. Whenever possible, turn to this meditation to release stress and restore your vitality.

Miracle Message #30:

If my environment dictates my mood,
then my life will feel like a roller coaster.
The way to steady ground is through my breath.
#MiraclesNow

#31: BE THE LIGHTHOUSE.

We all remember how we felt when we heard the news about the Sandy Hook Elementary School shootings. I was in the midst of a 60-hour Kundalini yoga–teacher training, surrounded by a faithful yogi community and our teacher. When we heard the news, we were distraught. Most of the people in my training group were parents. I could see the terror on their faces. The room fell silent, and people began weeping. Then we turned to our teacher, Gurmukh, for guidance. Gurmukh has dedicated the past 45 years of her life to Kundalini. She looked fondly at the class and spoke simple words that resonated with me deeply. She said, "You must not be the victim, you must be the lighthouse." We were empowered and moved by her response.

By no means was she suggesting that we ignore our feelings about the situation. Instead, she was guiding us to feel our feelings and use them to rise above the trauma. Rather than sit around in tears and fear, Gurmukh guided us in group prayer. We sat in a circle with our elbows against our ribs and our palms facing upward (as seen in the picture). In this circle we chanted the mantra *Ra Ma Da Sa Sa Se So Hung*, which means "I am Thou." It can also mean "the service of God is within me." This meditation can be done alone or in a group for self-healing and to heal others and the world. Those who practice this meditation participate in changing the vibration of the world.

Practice this meditation by yourself or in a group.

Posture: Sit cross-legged in Easy Pose (as seen in the picture).

Arms: Place your arms against your ribs with your hands held horizontally so your palms are facing upward.

Mantra: Chant *Ra Ma Da Sa Sa Se So Hung.* (Visit Gabbyb .tv/Miracles-Now to download the music and mantra.)

If you're in a group, sit in a circle with your hands facing one another to create a golden chain that connects the entire group. As a group, chant the mantra *Ra Ma Da Sa Sa Se So Hung.* You will feel an immediate shift in your energy and a great interconnectedness to the Universe.

You can do the same practice on your own.

If you're reading this book today, then whether you realize it or not, you have made the commitment to be the lighthouse. Anyone who is guided to a spiritual path will shift the consciousness of the world. Practice this meditation whenever you're stuck in fear and victimhood, and remember that the world needs your light.

Miracle Message #31:

I am not the victim. I am the lighthouse.

#MiraclesNow

#32: BATHE YOURSELF IN LIGHT.

When it comes to living a life of vitality, one of the most crucial tools is to learn how to recharge your energy. Often we get stuck in the mentality that we're not accomplishing anything if we're not overwhelmed and stressed. It's ironic when you consider the fact that overwhelm only slows us down by stealing all our energy. While we can't avoid overwhelm altogether, we can use tools that help us restore our energy and reboot.

One of my greatest tools for restoring my energy is to bathe in warm light. I know this sounds heady, but it's incredibly powerful! Find a quiet space in your home, in your gym's sauna, or even in your office (with the door locked). Lie down on the floor and envision a waterfall of light pouring over your body. Breathe deeply in and out of your nose. As you breathe, allow yourself to sink deeper and deeper into the floor. Continue to envision this waterfall of light pouring over you, calming you, cleansing you, and restoring you.

You may begin to feel your body actually vibrate and tingle. This is just a sign that your energy is recalibrating with the energy of the Universe. Remember, we are just energy surrounded by more energy. Quantum physics suggests that as you look deeply into the structure of the atom, you see that all that is there are just energy waves. We are made up of atoms that are continuously giving off, and absorbing, light and energy—even while we sleep.

When you understand that the body is made up of energy alone, you can see how depleting it is to feel stressed out and overwhelmed. Think of your body as a battery that can be recharged by positive energy. When we calm down and center our energy, we begin to vibrate with the powerful forces that surround us. Give your body a one-minute light bath that will recharge your battery.

Miracle Message #32:

Lie down and recharge your battery.
The world needs your energetic light.

#MiraclesNow

#33: LEAVE A POWERFUL ENERGY IMPRESSION.

Even if you're a chatterbox like me, the truth is that your energy speaks louder than your words, so understanding the power of your energy and thoughts is important. Many people take it for granted—they think that if they say and do all the right things, people will like them. But we all pick up on each other's energy; even if it happens only on a subconscious level, we can tell when someone's words or actions don't reflect their energy. It's important to accept the power of your thoughts and feelings in order to learn how to leave a positive and powerful energy impression.

Before you enter any environment where you'll be sharing your energy with others, use the following exercise for clearing your energy field and enhancing your magnetism. Start by taking a deep, full breath, expanding your diaphragm, and on the exhale, release the breath while your diaphragm contracts. Continue this cycle of deep breathing as you clear your mind and set positive intentions. Say to yourself, "I choose to remove any negative energy I've been holding onto. I choose to retrieve all the positive energy around me and within me. My intention is to share my positive energy with the world." With your breath and positive intentions, you can completely shift your mood and set yourself up to share your greatness with everyone you meet.

Leaving a positive energy impression will serve you in many ways. While it can greatly help you in connecting with others, the most important benefit is that you will feel a greater sense of support and life-flow. This principle will help you clear your energy before you enter a new situation so that you can always leave a positive impression.

Practice this the next time you enter a room. Whether you're meeting with someone you know very well or with a complete stranger, simply test-drive this exercise so you can access it at all times.

Miracle Message #33:

My positive energy leaves a powerful impression on the world.

#MiraclesNow

#34: BE A LOVE MACHINE.

Do you ever catch yourself judging people you don't even know—such as the person on the subway who's taking up two seats? Or do you feel like an outsider in certain environments, maybe your office, and project negative thoughts onto everyone so you can "protect" yourself from feeling hurt? Though your judgment may offer you temporary relief, it never actually makes you feel better in the long run.

When we separate ourselves from others, we disconnect from our loving truth and we feel blocked. The quickest and most effective way to bust through this block is to send love to all. Now, I'm not suggesting you go up to strangers on the bus and hug them. Instead, I'm offering you the opportunity to extend loving thoughts and energy to everyone you see.

As you learned from technique #32, you leave a powerful energy impression, good or bad, everywhere you go. So let's get into the practice of not only emanating love but actively sharing it, too.

Throughout the day, send love to everyone you see. You can send love through a thoughtful prayer, a smile, or the simple intention to be kind. If you're on the bus, subway, or even stuck in traffic, send love to your fellow commuters. You can say in your mind, *I pray for you to have a blessed day.* Before you walk into your work environment, silently bless everyone in the office. And when you come home at night to your roommates or family or even your cat, say a prayer for them before you walk in the door.

A Course in Miracles teaches us that prayer is the medium of miracles. Through a simple prayer of love, you can change someone's whole day. They may not know that you were doing something, but they will feel it for sure!

Yogi Bhajan said, "If you can't see God in all, you can't see God at all." Consider "God" to be the same as love. If you want to experience divine love in your life, practice seeing love in all. Think of yourself as a love machine that becomes more loving as love is spread.

Spread the love far and wide, and pay attention to how it makes you feel. Also pay attention to the way people react to you. Through a prayer, smile, or positive thought, you can change someone's life.

Miracle Message #34:

"If you can't see God in all,
you can't see God at all." — Yogi Bhajan

#YogiBhajan #MiraclesNow

#35: SURRENDER YOUR OBSESSIONS.

Have you ever wanted an outcome so badly that it became an obsession? Maybe you want that raise at work, or maybe you're consumed by the desire to find a romantic partner. There's nothing wrong with wanting something to happen, but obsessing about the outcome can drag you down fast.

When you're obsessing over an outcome, often friends will say, "Just let it go." As we all know, it's not that easy to *just let it go.* Sometimes we need to make an extra effort and surrender on a deeper level. Through genuine surrender you can release all outcomes and trust that the Universe has your back.

For years I've had a practice of surrendering my desires to a holy triangle. On my wall is a wooden triangle that is an emblem of the medium John of God from Brazil. Each side of the triangle represents a different idea: courage, faith, and hope. Whenever I have a desire that I cannot release, I write a note to the Universe and put it in the triangle. I'll write, *Thank you, Universe, for guiding this desire to _____ . I surrender this to you and I trust your plan is much better than mine.* Then I place the note in the triangle and leave it there for a week. Once the week is up, I take the desire out and burn it. (If burning your desire is in any way dangerous due to your surroundings, just flush it down the toilet!)

This simple act of writing a letter to the Universe and placing it in the holy triangle has helped me release some serious obsessions. Once it's in the triangle, stillness sets in and I immediately feel at peace.

You can make your own triangle or simply create a little God box by decorating a shoe box or jewelry case. The same way I place my desires in the triangle, you can place yours in a box. Either will do the trick. The Universe knows what's up and will take care of the rest.

Miracle Message #35:

I surrender my desires and I know the Universe has my back.

#MiraclesNow

#36: MOVE THROUGH THE BLOCKS.

In my book *Add More ~ing to Your Life*, I shared my love for rebounding on a mini trampoline. This fabulous exercise not only makes me feel more childlike and greatly supports the lymphatic system, it also helps me bust through blocks.

Whenever I'm sitting at my desk experiencing writer's block or feeling overwhelmed by the hundreds of unread e-mails in my inbox, I jump on my trampoline. Within one minute my body begins to shake off stress. I recommend 10 minutes for maximum vitality and peace. There are a few trampolines I like, which you can find at Gabbyb.tv/Miracles-Now.

If you don't want to purchase a trampoline or don't have space for one, simply jump rope or dance around your room. Gabrielle Roth, the founder of 5Rhythms dance, said, "Dance is the fastest, most direct route to the truth." Sometimes when I really need to shake things off, I turn on a powerful song and dance.

The human body needs to move. Research shows that jumping (ideally on the trampoline) is one of the most effective exercises because of how it benefits the lymphatic system. Think of the lymphatic system as the body's washing machine. It carries nutrients to the cells while leading away waste products. Movement is imperative for the lymphatic system to work properly. Without the proper movement, it gets blocked, leaving the cells to soak in waste without nutrients. This stagnation in the body can lead to cancer, arthritis, degenerative diseases, and aging.

The lymphatic system moves in one direction. The primary lymph vessels move up the legs, up the arms, and up the torso. This is why the vertical up and down movement on the trampoline is so helpful for pumping it. And if you usually wear tight clothes while working out, you'll want to skip them this time—in fact, you shouldn't even wear a bra. When I jump on my trampoline, I do it without a bra. The free movement of the breasts helps move the lymph through the breast tissue. I know this may sound crazy, but it's vital to our health.

Bounce, jump, dance—do whatever it takes to move the tension out of your body. Simple vertical movements can help you release the blocks within your mind and body. You don't need any specific amount of time or a certain type of clothing: All you need is the willingness to move through the blocks.

Miracle Message #36:

When I move my body, I bust through all that blocks me from my true health and vitality.

#MiraclesNow

#37: SHARE YOUR LIGHT
WITH THE WORLD.

You probably don't talk up your own awesomeness on a regular basis—if ever. Most of us, especially women, have been taught to see anything more than "quiet" confidence as boasting. In many cases the brighter we shine, the more negative reactions we receive: Maybe your big promotion made you the target of office gossip, or you became a Pilates rock star and were met with more backhanded compliments than congratulations. These kinds of experiences lead us to lose sight of our talents and inner spark, which in turn deprives the world of our greatness.

But when you play down your greatness out of fear that other people will be turned off by it, you forget how bright you can shine. Turn your inner spark into a blazing fire of greatness with these four tips. Weave them into your day—each one takes very little time, but the results will be immense.

Tip 1: Look inward. Our culture prizes external markers of success: the impressive job title, the decadently expensive wedding, the designer wardrobe (in the "right" size). But focusing on what's outside yourself totally blocks your inner light and can lead straight to low self-esteem. Remind yourself that what's beautiful about you has nothing to do with anything external to you. When you feel yourself getting caught up in "outside" stuff, simply meditate. Sit in stillness for one to three minutes and focus on your breath. You'll feel more grounded, more connected to yourself, and ready to shine.

Tip 2: Get real. Owning your quirks—like the fact that you can recite every episode of *Friends* or have an offbeat sense of humor—can be hard at first. Let's face it: not conforming takes guts, even once we're many years out of school. But there is nothing cooler or greater than your authentic truth, from the serious to the silly. The next time you have an opportunity to say what's on your mind, show your vulnerable side, or even ask for what you want. The more you embrace your real personality, the easier it will become. And letting your truth shine will let you feel more connected to others—they'll drop the pretenses and get real, too.

Tip 3: Actually make time for what you love. One brilliantly simple way to access your inner spark is to focus on what inspires you. Maybe you love to take photographs, but your camera's been gathering dust for months. Maybe you adore cooking, but have been so wrapped up in other stuff lately that your recycling bin has been filled with takeout containers. Commit to setting aside time every week (or even every day) to do what you love.

If you're not sure what inspires you, just pay attention to the things you do effortlessly, just because you love them. It could be as simple as writing in your journal or trying out a new hairstyle on a friend who's happy to let you experiment. You're good at so many things—you just have to learn how to see them.

Tip 4: Shine like you mean it! Share your talents and favorite finds with others. Knit a scarf for your favorite neighbor. Post your expertly crafted playlist to Facebook. E-mail friends that short story you wrote. These small actions aren't arrogant, nor are they intrusive. You're just sharing what makes you happy—and, in turn, inviting others to do the same. When your relatives, friends, or co-workers praise you, accept it with a simple, heartfelt "thank you." And don't be afraid to dish out compliments sincerely and liberally, too.

Miracle Message #37:

When I shine bright
I give others permission to shine with me.

#MiraclesNow

#38: SEE THE TORMENTOR
AS THE MENTOR.

There are probably people in your life who really push your buttons—the ones who make you feel twitchy every time you encounter them, such as the childhood pal who knows how to rev up your insecurities or the parent who can drive you over the edge within five minutes of saying hello. No matter how difficult these people may seem, they are your greatest teachers. Though this concept may baffle you at first, consider the possibility that you have something to learn here. As we've been exploring throughout this book, whenever you encounter an obstacle, there are opportunities to learn and grow. So how can you begin to see your tormentors as mentors?

The exercise is simple: Whenever your "tormentor" gets under your skin, instead of rushing to defend yourself or mount a takedown of whatever they've said, take a moment to breathe deeply. After three long, deep breaths, say to yourself, *What can I learn from this?* Open your consciousness to receive guidance on what can be learned from the situation. The feelings that others ignite in you are feelings that must come to the surface. Rather than push them down and blame the other person for driving you nuts, pay attention to what's coming up. If something is triggered, then something needs to be healed.

Once you've asked yourself what you can learn from the situation, take a minute to sit in stillness. Allow your subconscious to open you up to receive information. It's very possible that your intuition will speak loudly and offer you guidance. Maybe you'll hear a word such as "release," "love," or "forgive." Honor the intuitive hits you receive.

If you don't get any guidance in that minute of stillness, then pay attention to what comes up subtly throughout the day. You may hear a song that leads you to release pent-up anger or notice a tweet that offers you the exact message you need to hear. Guidance comes in many forms and is available to us all. We just need to ask for it and look out for the signs.

If you're dealing with a truly difficult person, sometimes the first lesson is simply tolerance and patience. It may take time to approach love and forgiveness, but taking that first step toward learning to tolerate others and be patient with them can help you shake off resentment and anger and turn torment into mentorship.

Miracle Message #38:

I can see the tormentor as the mentor.

#MiraclesNow

#39: JUST SHOW UP.

Confession: I don't always practice what I preach. There are plenty of days when I blow off my exercise or shorten my meditation. My ego resists personal growth and spirituality practice as much as anyone else's. I can easily get sucked into the ego's trap of laziness and avoidance, but it never makes me feel good.

We all experience apathy in our personal growth practices. Whether we're walking to the donut shop instead of the gym or avoiding our therapist for months, we're being affected by resistance of some kind. A great excuse is not having enough time. Often people say to me, "I don't have time to meditate," or "I don't have time to pray." My response is, "Do you have time to feel like shit?" The truth is, when you dedicate time to your personal growth, you wind up saving time—because you're not wasting a ton of it wallowing in crappy feelings. If you're ready to get unstuck and move out of the funk, this principle is your guiding light.

Something that greatly helped me with my occasional apathy was a suggestion I received from one of my Kundalini yoga teachers. He told me that the Kundalini masters suggested that 90 percent of the practice was just showing up to class or sitting on the mat. The act of showing up is a massive statement to the Universe that you are ready, willing, and able to receive guidance. Showing up supports you in creating a new habit and getting unstuck.

So if you've been avoiding the gym, don't freak out about what you'll do or how you'll feel once you get there—just lace up your sneakers and show up! Or if you've been neglecting your meditation practice, then hit the pillow and get your Om on. Whenever you catch yourself aimlessly scrolling through your Twitter feed, watching reruns, or wandering in and out of shops seeking a diversion, snap yourself out of your daze and seize the opportunity to leap out of your rut.

Whatever you've been apathetic about, make a point to just do it. Stop waiting for something major to happen—just show up for change.

Miracle Message #39:

Ninety percent of the practice of creating new habits is just showing up.

#MiraclesNow

#40: MEDITATE TO HEAL ADDICTION.

In some form or another, we all suffer from addiction. Some people choose drugs or alcohol, while others are hooked on food, sex, work, the Internet—the list is long. We turn to these substances or activities in an effort to avoid feeling our discomfort. Even if we're not addicted to traditional vices such as cigarettes and alcohol, we can be addicted subconsciously to neurotic patterns: fear, rejection, victimhood, and so on.

When we're addicted, there is an imbalance in the pineal gland (also called the third eye). The pineal gland is a small endocrine gland in the vertebrate brain. When the pineal gland is imbalanced, bad habits turn into severe addictions. The imbalance in the pineal gland affects the pituitary gland, which regulates the rest of the glandular system. When the pituitary gland is affected, the entire body and mind swing out of balance.

This meditation can be healing for anyone, but it's particularly helpful for people who are severely addicted and those in addiction recovery of any kind. Use this meditation for any type of dependency, from alcoholism to addiction to fear-based thoughts.

Follow the guidelines here and use the picture as an aid. This meditation is adapted from Yogi Bhajan's teaching.

Posture: Sit in an Easy Pose (cross-legged on the floor). Straighten the spine.

Eyes: Keep the eyes closed and focus at the brow point.

Mantra: *Saa Taa Naa Maa*

Mudra: Make fists of both hands and extend the thumbs straight. Place the thumbs on the temples and find the niche where the thumbs just fit. Lock the back molars together and keep the lips closed. Keeping the teeth pressed together throughout, alternately squeeze the molars tightly and then release the pressure. A muscle will move in rhythm under the thumbs. Feel it massage the thumbs and apply a firm pressure with the hands. Silently vibrate the five primal sounds—the Panj Shabd—*Saa Taa Maa Naa*, at the brow (as seen in the picture).

Time: Continue for 5 to 7 minutes. With practice, the time can be increased to 20 minutes and ultimately to 31 minutes.

This meditation can help heal any type of addiction. Practice it for 40 days or more—repeating it will help you break through your addictive patterns and set you free.

Miracle Message #40:

I am not my addictive patterns.
I am happy. I am free.

#MiraclesNow

#41: HANDLE FEAR IN THE WAKE OF A TERRIFYING EVENT.

When terrifying things happen in the world you may feel fearful, even if you live thousands of miles away. How do we handle our fears in these situations? It's easy to hide in a bar, numb out with the Internet, or turn off the news and pretend like nothing happened. But if you avoid your fear it will just haunt your subconscious. When tragedies occur, there is an emotional impact that sticks around until it is healed.

There's no one right or wrong way to handle our feelings, though there are tools that can help. Move through these three steps to honor, cope with, and heal your fear and pain.

Step 1: Get honest about your fear. It's healthy to admit you're afraid. When you honestly acknowledge your fear, you release the tension caused by holding onto it. Discuss your fear with a loved one, write about it in a journal, or share your experience with a therapist or a support group. Openly admitting your fear is a crucial step toward working through it.

Step 2: Breathe through your feelings. The next step is to identify where you carry fear in your body. You might hold it in your throat, your shoulders, your chest, or your stomach. Sit for a moment of stillness and sense where your body is holding fear. What part of you feels tense, tight, gnarled? Breathe deeply into that space. Continue to breathe into the tension and on the exhale, release it. Continue this cycle of breath until you feel the tension release. Your breath is your greatest tool for releasing fear in your body.

Step 3: Be more kind. The final step will help you more than you can imagine. Your kindness is the greatest power you have to heal the world. The more people who exercise kindness and compassion, the less destruction, terror, and attack will occur. From this point forward, show more kindness to everyone in your life, even strangers.

If you're feeling powerless, find your power now. Honor your feelings, breathe through the tension, and exercise your greatest virtue: kindness. Your true power lies in your capacity to love.

Miracle Message #41:

When I honor my feelings,
I find my power in powerless situations.
#MiraclesNow

#42: RESPECT YOUR MONEY AND YOUR MONEY WILL RESPECT YOU.

A dear friend of mine is an entrepreneur who often complained about feeling financially blocked. One day while she was complaining about her bills, she pulled out her wallet to pay for something. I gasped when I glanced at it. She was carrying around a tattered wristlet filled to the brim with credit cards, coins, crumpled receipts, lip gloss, and God knows what else. My immediate response was, "If you want to clean up your finances, you must clean up your wallet!"

One day later she texted me a picture of her shiny new red wallet. Each section was perfectly organized and she could easily find her money. Within two weeks her business was back in action and deals that had been held up for months were now closing. I believe it was the wallet. Once she had her personal money in order, she cleared subconscious blocks and was able to move freely and with ease in any situation related to finances or business.

Do you feel blocked financially? Is it far too often that the deal doesn't go through, the job doesn't work out, or you don't have enough money? Many times, a financial block stems from an energetic block. Remember, energy is in everything, even your wallet. For the sake of your finances and our economy, let's clean up your wallet to clear your energetic connection to receiving.

If your wallet is beat-up or overstuffed, buy a new one that's clean, beautiful, and can hold all you need to carry. Self-love blogger Gala Darling says, "Your wallet is a reflection of how you feel about money. So is your wallet ripped, tattered, or torn? Have you had the same one for twenty years? Start fresh." A wallet isn't just an accessory. It's where you store your money: Make sure you love it! Don't be afraid to invest in one that makes you feel good.

When picking out a new wallet, be mindful of its color. In the feng shui tradition, certain colors welcome abundance, such as gold, red, and green. Bust out the sparkly gold or the radiant red. Go big or go home with this one.

Feng shui expert Kate MacKinnon says, "Like everything in feng shui, the most important way to make space is to clear clutter. So make sure your wallet is clear of clutter (paper, receipts, etc.) and organized."

Not only will your new, clean wallet energetically support you, it will also make a statement to the Universe that you are ready to receive. Respect your money and your money will respect you.

Miracle Message #42:

Respect your money and
your money will respect you.

#MiraclesNow

#43: I CHOOSE PEACE INSTEAD OF THIS.

Throughout my journey of spiritual growth, one message from *A Course in Miracles* that always resonated with me deeply was "Only the mind decides on what it would receive and give." This point reminds me that in any given situation I have the choice to perceive love or to perceive fear. Through the daily practice of choosing love over fear, eventually love became an involuntary response. Of course, my fearful ego sneaks up on me often, but through perseverance, the loving voice now speaks louder.

Living a miraculous life takes commitment. In every given moment we have a divine spiritual assignment in front of us: Choose love or choose fear. Therefore, bring this concept with you throughout your day. In the moments when you witness yourself choosing fear, attack, judgment, and separation, simply say: "I choose to see peace instead of this." Make this your mantra.

When you choose love in any way, you're unconsciously connecting to your higher self, asking for love to reinterpret the situation. And yes, this affirmation is easy to apply when the issue isn't that difficult to deal with. But when you're hit with a heavy assignment, use this principle with even more conviction. Trust in its power and you'll see results you couldn't have imagined. *A Course in Miracles* says, "Miracles arise from conviction."

Practice this principle in all situations and heighten your commitment to miracles. In an instant you will feel peace set in.

Miracle Message #43:

When in doubt, say:
I choose to see peace instead of this.

#MiraclesNow

#44: START YOUR DAY ON THE RIGHT FOOT.

Your morning routine sets the tone for your entire day. If you're the type of person who snoozes beyond the limit, checks e-mail as soon as you get up, and then turns on the news while drinking a cup of coffee, it's likely you start the day with stress. No judgment, folks, but let's get real here. When you begin your day with stressors and stimulants, you set yourself up for a chaotic and taxing experience.

One of the key tools for living a life of flow is beginning your day on the right foot—literally. An age-old Kundalini technique suggests that you step out of bed on your dominant foot. How do you know which foot is dominant? Simply breathe out each nostril individually and see which side is stuffed and which is clear. Whichever side is the clearest is the side that you step out on. If your right nostril is breathing easy, step out on your right foot. I know this sounds silly, but it makes a tangible difference in how you start your day.

Once you're up and out of bed, DON'T turn to your e-mail, text messages, or news feed. Instead, begin with a positive affirmation. If you have an affirmation you love, recite it out loud or post it on your mirror. If you want guidance in this area, check out my Spirit Junkie alarm app at Gabbyb.tv/Spirit-Junkie-App. Rather than wake up to the jarring sounds of your alarm, kick off your day with beautiful tones and a positive affirmation that pops up on your screen. A positive thought first thing in the morning can carry you throughout the day. Your nervous system is very sensitive to your thoughts. Therefore, it's important to make sure the thoughts you have in the morning are loving and empowering, because they lay the foundation for the rest of your day.

Finally, before you leave the house, set a positive intention for the day. Intend to be kind to yourself and others. Intend to empower your co-workers, be creative, or be more forgiving. When you set positive intentions at the beginning of the day, you'll be totally hooked up.

Use these tools every morning and expect miracles.

Miracle Message #44:

I begin my day with gratitude and love.

#MiraclesNow

#45: LET PEACE BE
YOUR RESPONSE.

Sometimes the greatest lessons and tools come from the most unexpected circumstances. For instance, I often post "selfies" (self-portraits) on Instagram, Twitter, and Facebook. As an avid social media junkie I enjoy sharing my life and interacting with readers. However, with frequent posts often come negative comments. While revisiting an old Instagram post, I noticed there were tons of comments about a particular photo of me. I immediately checked them out and came to find a bunch of people aggressively reacting to the image by putting me down for sharing self-portraits and judging me for having a plant-based diet.

As I continued to scroll through the comments, I noticed a faithful Spirit Junkie follower respond with a quote from the journalist and critic Dream Hampton: "Face gossip with silence." I loved the message and felt my heart soften. This quote reminded me of one of the greatest lessons from *A Course in Miracles*: "In my defenselessness my safety lies." The *Course* reminds us that as we defend against the attacks of others we invest in their attack.

Fighting back against an attack creates more stress, drama, and angst. I'm not saying that you shouldn't stick up for yourself when necessary, but I am suggesting you try to remain silent in the face of this sort of attack. This may be tough at first because our ego's involuntary response is to fight back and protect ourselves. But think for a moment about how you feel when you're fighting back against an attack. It's likely that you get stressed, angry, and out of balance. If peace is your intention, let peace be your response.

The next time you feel attacked in any way, use this one-minute miracle to shift your perception and choose peace instead of fear. In an instant you can resolve all attack thoughts with love.

Miracle Message #45:

"Face gossip with silence." — Dream Hampton

#MiraclesNow

#46: MEASURE YOUR SUCCESS WITH HOW MUCH FUN YOU'RE HAVING.

Each New Year's Eve I practice a ritual of writing down my intentions for the year to come. For the past two years I've made the intention to measure my success with how much fun I'm having. I came to this intention after living the opposite way and hitting bottom. For a while I was measuring my success based on my level of stress, but then I surrendered to the fact that true success must be based on happiness.

It's easy to measure our success based on a dollar amount, a relationship status, or a job credential. But what I've learned is that nothing outside of us can make us feel truly happy. Happiness is an inside job. We can take pleasure in life's successes but we must focus on the greatest success of all: living a fun, fulfilling life.

It's our job to find the fun in everything. Some of the happiest people I know have the innate ability to find joy in the most joyless scenarios. Gurmukh, my Kundalini teacher whom I mentioned earlier, is a fantastic example. At 70 she exudes the innocence of a little girl, finding joy in everything and everyone. Her life is filled with joy regardless of her given circumstances.

What I've learned from Gurmukh is that her joyful state is a conscious choice. Even though she is a dedicated yogi she still has to commit to peace every single day. Maintaining a sense of joy is a moment-to-moment commitment. The energy of the world around us can take us out in an instant. Our job is to stay in the flow with joy.

To apply this principle in your own life, begin by making a commitment. Post this affirmation on your desk, mirror, car dashboard, or wherever you can see it often: *I measure my success by how much fun I'm having.* For the next 40 days, begin the day with this affirmation. Make the conscious commitment to choose joy upon waking. Throughout the day, consciously look for joy in all situations. Taste your food, feel the blessing of a smile from a stranger, become more curious about your surroundings. Establishing this new habit will greatly benefit your physical, emotional, and spiritual well-being.

You can start now by finding fun in each exercise of *Miracles Now*! Oftentimes people view personal growth work as a chore. Rather than make it difficult, make it joyous. When creating life changes we must exert more than just willpower—we must find joy in our transformation. Practice this principle all the time and you will live in joy.

Miracle Message #46:

I measure my success
by how much fun I'm having.

#MiraclesNow

#47: YOUR PRESENCE IS YOUR POWER.

Our ability to cope with stressors and adopt a positive stress response is called "allostasis." The body is capable of restoring its balance naturally, but when stressors take over they hijack our body's normal function. When we get too stressed, our stress response turns against us. This is called the "allostatic load."

When you experience allostatic load, it's likely that the world around you reflects your low-level energy. When stress takes over, life feels more blocked. Other people can sense our energy on a subconscious level, so in order to have free-flowing powerful relationships and experiences, we must have the tools to clear our energy field.

We are our presence and our presence is our power. The energy force that we bring to all situations and relationships is a direct reflection of what we will receive back. That energy force is our presence. Access your power presence by practicing the following meditation, which is called Breath of Fire with Lion's Paws. Yup, lion's paws! This short exercise (or *kriya*) has an immediate effect on the brain and on your electromagnetic field (presence of power). It is suggested that you practice this meditation for nine minutes, but even a one-minute practice will create an energetic shift.

Below is a breakdown of the meditation as taught by Yogi Bhajan. Reference the photo on page 112 for a visual image of how to practice this meditation. You can also visit Gabbyb.tv/Miracles-Now for the video breakdown.

Posture: Sit in Easy Pose, with a slight neck lock, your chin tucked down, and your tongue pushed close to the roof of the mouth *(jalandhar bandha)*.

Mudra: Curl and tighten the fingers of each hand (Lion's Paws). Keep the tension in the hands throughout the exercise. Extend both arms out to the sides, parallel to the ground with the palms up. The applied pressure in the hands triggers reflexes in the fingertips to each area of the brain. The movement of the arms moves the lymph in the lymphatic system. It also pressurizes the nervous system to change its current state.

Breath and Movement: Bring both arms up over the head so that the hands pass each other over the crown of the head. The elbows bend and the palms face down. Then bring the hands back down as you extend the arms out parallel to the ground again. Start a rhythmic motion in this way. Alternate which wrist is in front when they cross by each other over the head. Create a powerful breath with the motion of the arms. The arm motion is very fast paced. You inhale as the arms extend and exhale as the arms cross over the head. The breath becomes fast and steady. The breath added to the motion enhances the functioning of the pituitary and stimulates the pineal gland to increase the radiance and subtle frequency of the brain's projection.

Time: Continue for nine minutes. (Note: You can practice for one minute and still achieve great benefits.)

To End: Without breaking the pace of the exercise, stick the tongue out and down all the way. Continue for 15 seconds more.

Then inhale, bring in the tongue, and fix the arms at 60 degrees, so that they form an arc around the head with the palms facing down about six inches apart over the head. The hands are still in Lion's Paws. Hold the breath for 15 seconds.

Keep the arms fixed as you exhale and inhale completely. Then hold the breath for 30 seconds. Relax and let the arms down. Meditate at the Heart Center. Follow the gentle flow of the breath. Chant an inspiring and uplifting song. Continue for 3 to 5 minutes.

Practice this meditation to expand your presence and your inner power. The world needs your true strength, so don't be afraid to let it shine. If you feel you are experiencing the allostatic load, use this meditation to realign your energy field so you can dwell from a space of peace.

Miracle Message #47:

Your presence is your power.

#MiraclesNow

#48: RESOLVE INNER CONFLICT.

No matter how well things are going in your life, the ego still finds ways to create inner conflict. In fact, I've found that the happier I've become, the craftier my ego is. Everything can be going great in my life and then in an instant I can be taken down by some insane ego belief that spins me out of control.

A Course in Miracles teaches us, "I am never upset for the reason I think." All inner conflict stems from fear-based illusions that the ego so artfully places into our psyche. These fearful illusions show up time and time again unless we choose to become the master of our own mind.

Yogi Bhajan said, "If you master your mind, you master the whole Universe." Through Kundalini meditation we can be released of the ego's stronghold and release our attachment to the ego's fearful beliefs. Spiritual commitment can resolve inner conflict.

Today's technique is the powerful Kundalini meditation called "inner-conflict resolver." This practice will help you soften your ego and melt away any sense of separation. This heart-opening experience will help you hold and maintain an experience of compassion.

Inner Conflict Resolver Meditation

Sit comfortably in a chair or cross-legged on the floor.

Place your palms on your upper chest with your thumbs facing upward.

Breathe in your nose for five seconds.

Breathe out your nose for five seconds.

Hold your breath for 15 seconds.

Continue this cycle of breath for one minute (or as long as you wish).

Let your breath open your heart.

Let today's Miracle Message remind you that you can choose to release inner conflict by following your spiritual path.

Miracle Message #48:

My spiritual practice can resolve all inner conflict.

#MiraclesNow

#49: SHIELD YOURSELF FROM BAD ENERGY.

Ever feel really drained after spending time with someone—almost like they stole your energy? If you've had this type of encounter it's likely you've come across an energy vampire. These folks, often without realizing it, take your positive energy and leave a negative energetic imprint on you.

I know this must sound trippy, but it's important to understand. Every one of us is made up of energy, and as we flow in the cosmic universal energy field, we can easily pick up what other people are puttin' out! It's also easy for others to lift our good vibes. With this insight you can learn how to protect your own energy.

The first step is to become aware of the energy vampires in your life. Be mindful not to judge them or put them down. Remember, we're all doing the best we can. People who don't have any energy awareness are not evil or malicious; they're just struggling to get by. So rather than blame them, simply become mindful of the ways they may suck you dry or leave you with their negative load.

Start by making a list of the people who negatively affect your energy. To properly identify who's an energy vampire, you can check in about the following attributes:

- Do you feel tired or weak after spending time with them?

- Do you experience mild or even heavy depression when you leave their presence?

- Do they make you feel drained or lethargic?

If you answer these questions honestly, you'll quickly come to recognize the energy vampires in your life. Now let's create boundaries to protect your auric field, which is the energy field that surrounds you. Without judgment, begin to use this principle to support yourself.

Upon identifying the energy vampires in your life, make a conscious commitment to protect yourself whether you're physically around them or not. It's important to understand that energy cords between people can exist even when you're miles away.

Remember the light bath exercises? That same energizing light can protect you, too. Envision a shield of golden light surrounding you and protecting you. Whenever you think of this person or enter into their physical space, make sure to activate your light shield. I know this may sound a little heady, but trust me, it works. Your intentions create your experience, so if you intend to shield yourself from negativity, then you will no longer be a match for the bad vibes.

Each time you encounter someone who has placed a negative energy imprint on you, recite the following prayer: "I ask that any negative energy I picked up be removed, recycled, and transmuted. I ask that any positive energy I may have lost be retrieved now." The same way you can create powerful boundaries with your words, you can create even more powerful boundaries with your prayers.

Make it a practice to be aware of how other people's energy affects you. And don't forget the power your energy has on others: Be mindful of the imprints you leave.

Miracle Message #49:

By spreading loving energy,
I attract more love.

#MiraclesNow

#50: "LOVE WILL IMMEDIATELY ENTER INTO ANY MIND THAT TRULY WANTS IT."

A Course in Miracles teaches that miracles arise from conviction. Our conviction and commitment to love is what helps us continue to shine from the inside out.

To live a miraculous life we must stay committed to miracles. As we waver in and out of fear, it's easy to get hooked into the ego's illusions about the world. We each have specific areas of our lives that can trigger our fears. For some of us it's money, for others it's romance or body image, and so on. If we want to sustain our miracle mind-set and live with ease, we must proactively choose love as often as possible.

Are you ready to deepen your commitment even more? Our guiding message today comes from the *Course*: "Love will immediately enter into the mind that truly wants it." Now that you've established more discipline in your spiritual practice, it's time to heighten your aware-ness of when the ego distracts you from miracles. Use this message whenever you're in doubt. Proactively remind yourself, "Love will immediately enter into the mind that truly wants it." Use this affirmation all the time and then in an instant make a decision to *want love* over fear. Your desire is your conviction and miracles arise from that.

Become more and more committed to miracles as each day progresses. Let each miracle add up as you move into the second half of this book. Each new day brings opportunities to learn, grow, and strengthen your faith in love.

Miracle Message #50:

"Love will immediately enter into any mind that truly wants it."
— *A Course in Miracles*
#ACIM #MiraclesNow

#51: LET PEOPLE RANT
IF THEY WANT TO!

I often listen to Dr. Christiane Northrup's radio show, and I always pick up incredible wisdom and advice. On one show, a caller complained that her mother loved to rant about how miserable she was. The caller went on to say, "My mother hates life and doesn't believe in happiness."

When I heard this comment, my curiosity was piqued—how would Dr. Northrup answer? Without hesitation she responded, "Then just let her rant!" She went on to explain that when people insist on living in fear, our job isn't to transform them. Instead, a powerful tool for dealing with negative people is to just let them be negative. Dr. Northrup suggested that when the other person wants to complain you let them, and even go as far as to engage in the negativity. You can say things like, "I know how hard this must be for you. This really sucks." And so on. It may seem counterintuitive—but reinforcing their negativity can help nudge them toward a more helpful experience. They may feel a sense of relief because they no longer need to defend their bad attitude. Or they may experience a breakthrough moment in which they actually witness the illusion of their negativity. Regardless of the outcome, this practice will help the other person truly experience their negativity.

This practice will not only support the other person but it will greatly help you. When we resist the negativity of others we start to feel negative. But when we allow the negativity to rise and pass, we can be the observer rather than a sponge soaking up their bad vibes. Test-drive this exercise the next time you're around someone who wants to rant, and enjoy the uplifting results.

Miracle Message #51:

Allowing people to witness their behavior can help them move beyond it.

#MiraclesNow

#52: MEDITATE TO RELEASE IRRATIONALITY.

Ever find yourself in such emotional distress that you become irrational? I admit I can go there from time to time—such as when I feel exhausted or frustrated by an outcome, or if I skip my daily Sadhana (spiritual practice). It's easy to spin out of control and lose it on a loved one (or a stranger!).

One issue with being irrational is that, deep down, you know your inner drama queen is coming out. Even if your ego wants to act out, your higher self knows you're far cooler than that. So it's a lose-lose all around—it's likely you piss people off and subconsciously feel like a petulant child. Rather than let your ego get the best of you, practice this meditation often to calm your mind, soothe your nerves, and protect you from irrationality.

This Kundalini meditation is called Backpack Meditation #3. You can use this one anytime and anywhere. It's also a fabulous stress buster and it will help you maintain a calm vibe.

Backpack Meditation #3

Sit comfortably cross-legged in Easy Pose on the floor.

The mudra for this meditation is different for men and women. If you're a woman, place your left hand at your ear with your thumb and ring finger touching. Then gently place your right hand in your lap with thumb tip and little finger touching. If you're a man, reverse the hands but use the same mudra. (As seen in the picture here.)

Your eyes should be one-tenth open like a crescent moon. Your breath should be long, deep, and relaxed. It is suggested that you sit in this meditation for 11 to 31 minutes, though like all the meditations in this book, even 1 minute will make a difference.

At the end of the meditation, raise your hands over your head and shake them rapidly for several minutes. I suggest playing the Florence + the Machine song, "Shake It Out." You can get a really fun boogie going and shake out all your toxic energy.

You can use this meditation when you're stuck in an irrational rut or you can practice it daily to maintain a calm and balanced vibe. Use it however you wish and enjoy the soothing results.

Miracle Message #52:

I can find peace in every breath.

#MiraclesNow

#53: VALUE YOURSELF AND THE WORLD WILL VALUE YOU.

My dear friend Kate Northrup, the author of *Money, A Love Story*, has taught me so much about valuing myself. Kate has made it her mission to teach others how to value their strengths so that the world can reflect that value back to them. She offered this powerful tool for heightening your power to value yourself.

Here's the exercise, straight from Kate:

> Right now, think of three specific things you value about yourself. Saying, "I'm healthy" as something you value about yourself is great, but it doesn't stir the same emotional response as when you're really specific. For example, I could say, "I have strong, toned legs that get me from place to place" as something I value about myself. Yes, it's related to my health, but it's more specific and immediately makes me feel more valuable than simply saying "I'm healthy."

Make this a habit. When you begin or end the day by writing down three specific things you value about yourself (all different from what you wrote down the day before), you'll create a profound shift not only in how you feel about yourself, but also in the way you show up in the world. People who value themselves attract people who value them, too. And people who value themselves are filled up emotionally and are able to give more value to others.

Tempted to repeat something from the day before? Don't! I promise, there's an infinite supply of reasons you're amazing and truly valuable, so finding three new ones each day is not only possible, it will also become fun and easy as you form the habit.

Take Kate's suggestion and begin a daily practice of acknowledging reasons that you value yourself. You'll be amazed by the way the world responds to your new sense of self-love and respect. Remember, the outside world is just a reflection of your internal condition. So by empowering your inner life, you receive powerful love from the world.

Miracle Message #53:

"People who value themselves attract people who value them, too." — Kate Northrup

#MiraclesNow

#54: THERE IS ALWAYS A SOLUTION OF THE HIGHEST GOOD.

I try my best to stay faithful to the belief that there is always a solution of the highest good. This concept is easy to trust when everything is working out in your favor. But when the Universe throws you a curveball, it's also easy to lose faith in the midst of discomfort. Instead we look for more problems or people to blame.

What I've come to learn and accept is that there *is* always a solution of the highest good—even though it may not be aligned with what I think is right. My job is to stay faithful to miracles and choose the highest good nonetheless. I've found that the more I commit to this perspective, the easier it is to move through uncomfortable situations. For instance, a coaching client of mine struggles with her relationship with her sister. In this relationship jealousy and competition are at an all-time high. My client spent years defensive and filled with anger. Though her ego was driving the fear train, she committed to having faith that there was a solution of the highest good. She continued to allow herself to be guided. As time went on, her sister's insistence remained steady, but my client's fear weakened. While the outside circumstances didn't change, her internal circumstances did. She began to witness how she was calmer and much less reactive about the situation. She began to open up to forgiveness and she even had dreamed of being at peace with her sister. Because she kept the door open for the spiritual solution, the spiritual solution showed up.

In my client's case, the solution wasn't a clear direction but rather an unconscious release of resentment and fear. Your situation may be different—you might see the solution as a clearly guided direction that leads to peace. But the form of the solution doesn't matter. You don't need to worry about the solution you receive; instead, simply be open to receive whatever is of the highest good. When you are dealing with a difficult situation, this short affirmation will help you keep the faith: *There is always a solution of the highest good.* Recite it silently or out loud when you're confronted with struggle, and you'll keep the door open to receive. Your openness is all you need.

Miracle Message #54:

There is always a solution of the highest good.

#MiraclesNow

#55: TURN YOUR TENSION UPSIDE DOWN.

One afternoon I was hanging out with my friend Jenny in my office (which also acts as a yoga Zen den). Out of nowhere Jenny popped up into a headstand. Jenny's an avid yogi known for her love of the practice—but I was still taken a bit by surprise. While upside down, Jenny explained that doing headstands helps turn her mood around. Whenever she feels stagnant or blocked, doing some kind of inversion gets her energy moving and greatly supports her transition into a higher state of consciousness.

So rather than watch her while she revitalized her energy, I decided to join in on the action. I went into a headstand against the wall for support. Within a minute I felt an energy rush. All my energy seemed to be literally turned upside down and I started to feel more alive.

I now make inversions a daily routine. In addition to the supported headstand, I also do Plow Pose. Both of these inversions are pretty easy to move into whenever you need a boost. I find Plow Pose a lot easier for people who are new to yoga. You can do this pose on your bedroom floor, outside on the grass, or anywhere there is a soft surface. (**Note:** If you have back, neck, or any structural problems, please skip this exercise.)

Plow Pose

To get into Plow Pose, lie on your back and bring your spine and legs up to a vertical position, supporting your butt with your arms. Your shoulders and elbows support your body weight (get your legs as vertical as you can and make sure that all of your weight is on your shoulders, not on your neck). Next, bend your knees and set your feet against the floor. Exhale and push your feet away from the floor, drawing your legs up in the air so you're standing on your shoulders. Then from there, exhale and bend from the hip joints to slowly lower your toes to the floor behind your head. Keep your torso perpendicular to the floor and your legs fully extended. Lightly drop your toes to the floor and lift your thighs and tailbone toward the ceiling. Draw your chin away from the sternum and soften your throat.

To enhance the posture, you can press your hands against the back torso and press your back up toward the ceiling. You can use your hands for support or you can release them away from your back and stretch the arms out behind you on the floor.

To exit the pose, drop your hands onto your back again and raise your legs into a shoulder stand and exhale your way down to the ground.

Practice an inversion for one minute or more and you will receive great benefits. This simple practice can turn your bad mood, stress, or foggy mind upside down and recharge your energy. Inversions increase blood flow and improve concentration, memory, and awareness.

Inversions also improve digestion and elimination—many yogis suggest inversions to overcome constipation. Another health benefit of inversions is that they promote lymphatic drainage and blood purification. The lymphatic system clears toxins from the tissues and supports your overall immunity. The reason you feel so rejuvenated after an inversion is because the pose is detoxifying.

Most important, inversions will lift your spirit and relieve depression. When you increase your circulation and send oxygen to the brain, you release neurotransmitters and endorphins while balancing your hormones.

Turn your blocks upside down with an inversion for one minute (or more) a day.

Miracle Message #55:

An inversion a day keeps stress at bay.

#MiraclesNow

#56: GIVE MORE OF WHAT YOU WANT TO RECEIVE.

Often what we want most is something we're not giving. Maybe you're looking for more love but you've been
walking around feeling unlovable. Or possibly you want
to receive more money but you've been too afraid to do-
nate to charity or share with friends in need. When you
withhold anything, you cut off an important energy exchange. The simple truth is that what you energetically
put out, you will receive back. When you focus your attention on what you're giving, then the energy you give off is
loving and joyful. That joyful energy you give off is what
attracts more to you.

Giving more of what you want doesn't mean that you
have to only give something tangible. Simply giving off
certain energy will attract more of that energy into your
life. For instance, if you feel abundant (regardless of your
financial situation) you will attract more abundance. Or,
if you feel love and romance (even if you're single) you will
attract more love and romance into your life.

Take a close look at what you've been longing to receive and ask yourself, *Is this something I'm not giving?* Are
you wishing for that romantic partner while walking
around feeling alone and sad? Or do you want a new job,
but you're telling everyone that you're not worthy of it?
Take an honest inventory; you'll come to see how your

energy and actions have been reflected back to you. Be fearless yet gentle with yourself.

Once you're clear about what you've been withholding, it's time to give it. Give the love you've been denying, give the forgiveness to the person you've been resenting, give the attention to the health you've been ignoring. Give what you want to receive and feel your energy shift. Giving off more positivity in any area of your life will blast open the doors to happiness—and to receiving.

A Course in Miracles teaches: "Miracles are teaching devices for demonstrating it is as blessed to give as to receive. They simultaneously increase the strength of the giver and supply strength to the receiver." Give knowing that peace will be bestowed upon you whenever you extend peace to others.

Miracle Message #56:

Give more of what you want to receive.

#MiraclesNow

#57: SURRENDER IT ALL.

Most of my crazy obsessions are over the little things—
such as whether I should change a flight time or resched-
ule an appointment. I can drive myself batty pondering
those small matters! But when something major is happening in my life, like a career opportunity or a family
issue, I never fail to hit my knees and surrender. I find it
easier to have faith in the big stuff than in the little stuff.

One major reason for that is that our logical minds
often thinks they can control the little things. We feel
comforted by a sense of agency and responsibility, but
that comfort quickly turns into frustration when we realize we don't actually have the control we crave. I've come
to learn that I cannot hold on to anything—especially the
small stuff. Surrendering it all is crucial to my happiness.

You may be thinking, "Well that sounds great, but
how in the hell can I surrender *everything?*"

Don't sweat it: That's the reaction I expect! The ego
wants to hold on to everything, so the concept of letting go
will probably freak you out. But the purpose of this principle is to simply become *willing* to surrender everything.

Here's an example of what happens to me when I try
to control my life and then finally surrender. I often get
hung up on trying to control my travel schedule. I flip
out over making decisions and changing flights. My ego
will go wild making up reasons for me to freak out, which
causes my blood pressure and stress hormones to spike.
I'll go a full day feeling panicked over a decision that I

could make quite easily if I were in a more peaceful state. After hours of stressing and obsessing, I'll hit my knees and pray. The moment I pray I feel a sense of relief. Even if it's fleeting, it's enough. The simple prayer opens the door for me to receive new information and guidance. Within minutes I may get the intuition to call a friend who can support me, or sometimes a friend will call me before I even pick up the phone. *A Course in Miracles* says, "The secret of true prayer is to forget the things you think you need." Once we fully surrender our agenda, we can allow the guidance of the Universe to set in. A positive intention and a surrendered prayer can reorganize any situation toward an outcome of the highest good.

Though I remember to pray, it's often after hours or sometimes days of anxiety. Most of us come to a place of surrender at some point, but why wait hours, days, or weeks? We can surrender *all the time* with a simple prayer. When we take that moment to surrender our will, we invite a presence greater than us to take over. Yogi Bhajan said, "When we fold our hands in prayer, God opens His arms and gives us a hug." This message says it all. When in doubt, fold your hands and pray.

Though prayer seems passive, it is very active. When we pray we're consciously setting the intention to see things differently. That is the miracle. Our conscious commitment to release our control shifts our energy and brings us to a peaceful state in which we can receive new information, and that is how we are guided. We can only experience this guidance if we ask for it.

The practice of prayer will be emphasized throughout this book. For many people new to a spiritual path, prayer may seem strange. To have a prayer practice you don't need to get on your knees and recite a religious text. All you need to do is "let go of what you think you need" and surrender. Pray whenever you're indecisive, overly obsessing, or caught in a fear spiral. Try not to pray for a specific outcome—instead, pray for peace. Accessing a peaceful state of mind is all we really need.

Miracle Message #57:

I surrender it all.

#MiraclesNow

#58: TAP ON PAIN.

We're bringing tapping back—this time, we will tap on pain. We all are affected by physical pain in different ways. Whether it's a daily neck ache from hunching over a laptop, PMS cramps, or chronic pain from an injury, tapping can help you release it.

Sometimes our obsession over physical pain stems from an emotion. Our emotions trigger shifts in our bodies' delicate balance of hormones and neurotransmitters. Positive emotions support our health, while negative emotions stimulate stress hormones such as adrenaline and cortisol. Negative emotions are also a major contributor to pain. Therefore, tapping on your pain allows you to release your emotional attachment to it, thereby relieving the physical discomfort as well. If it sounds powerful, that's because it is!

Let's begin the process by identifying your Most Pressing Issue (MPI) around your pain. Maybe your MPI is something like, "I can't get through the day because of all this back pain." Or maybe something like, "The pain in my head is distracting me from life." Once you identify your MPI, rate it from 1 to 10 (10 being the most difficult). Once you've rated your MPI, we can begin tapping. Follow my tapping script and repeat each phrase out loud while tapping on the different meridians specified. Just follow my lead and expect miracles.

Start by tapping on the karate chop point, as shown on page 58. Tap lightly on each point approximately seven times. As you tap, repeat the following phrase or your MPI three times: *Even though it is a struggle to live with this pain, I deeply and completely love and accept myself.* Or follow the guidance from this video: Gabbyb.tv/Miracles-Now

Karate chop: *Even though it is a struggle to live with this pain, I deeply and completely love and accept myself.*

Karate chop: *Even though it is a struggle to live with this pain, I deeply and completely love and accept myself.*

Karate chop: *Even though it is a struggle to live with this pain, I deeply and completely love and accept myself.*

Start at the eyebrow point and tap the points down the face, and down to the under-arm point, then to the top of head. Start again at the eyebrow point. Tap one statement at each tapping point.

Eyebrow: *All this pain.*

Side of eye: *I can't live with it anymore!*

Under eye: *All this pain in my body.*

Under nose: *I'm so uncomfortable.*

Chin: *I don't like it.*

Collarbone: *I cannot move forward with my life.*

Under arm: *I can't stand being in pain.*

Top of head: *This pain is disturbing my life.*

Eyebrow: *It stops me from being at peace.*

Side of eye: *It blocks me from living life.*

Under eye: *Maybe this pain is trying to teach me something.*

Under nose: *I'd like to be open to that information.*

Chin: *I'm willing to learn from this pain.*

Collarbone: *Maybe there's something I need to take care of.*

Under arm: *Maybe there's a feeling I'm not expressing.*

Top of head: *Another pain I'm avoiding.*

Eyebrow: *Or it's distracting me from that bigger pain.*

Side of eye: *What if I could just feel the pain and let it go?*

Under eye: *I'm open to feeling the emotions that block me.*

Under nose: *What if I could relax now?*

Chin: *Some of this pain might be from stress and tension.*

Collarbone: *What if I were ready to let it all go?*

Under arm: *I give my body and mind permission to let go of this pain.*

Top of head: *Let go.*

Eyebrow: *I am allowing myself to relax.*

Side of eye: *I release my attachment to this pain.*

Under eye: *I am ready to let it go now.*

Under nose: *I want to be free and happy.*

Chin: *I choose to feel good.*

Top of head: *All is well.*

Take a gentle deep breath.

Now check in with your MPI and see where you rate it on a scale of 1 to 10. It's likely the rating has dropped—whether radically or just a few notches. If your MPI is still close to a 10, feel free to keep tapping.

Releasing your attachment to physical pain will greatly help you create more flow in your life and move forward with grace. Embrace all the guidance that comes through in the tapping process. You may come to realize that your physical pain is merely a manifestation of a deep-rooted emotional pain that needs to rise to the surface for healing. Be open to the guidance you receive and trust in the tapping process.

Miracle Message #58:

Underneath my physical pain is an emotional call for love.

#MiraclesNow

#59: HONOR YOUR COMMITMENTS.

For most of my adolescence, I was very selfish and cared only about my own priorities and schedule. I rarely honored my commitments. I couldn't stick to a plan or show up when I said I would. Due to this poor behavior, I ruined many relationships and lacked deep connections because I was so untrustworthy. Upon getting sober, I chose to make up for my behavior by honoring all my future commitments to the best of my ability. Today, many years into my sober recovery, I hold this commitment in high regard and love the feeling of showing up when I say I will.

There's an unconscious sense of guilt that comes over anyone who doesn't stick to plans or commitments. Whether you realize it or not, you probably don't like yourself very much when you blow people off. This guilt can block you from deepening relationships, creating new opportunities, and enhancing your life. And the solution couldn't be more straightforward: All you have to do is show up when you say you will. I understand that there are often legitimate reasons to change a plan, but when not showing up becomes the norm, it's time to change. This exercise will help you get clear about how you've been dishonoring yourself and others through a lack of commitment.

Get honest with yourself about how well you stick to your commitments. Make a list of all the ways you may flake, change plans, or reorganize your life so it suits you. Then write a list of how this behavior affects others. Finally, write down how it makes you feel.

Take a moment to look closely at your behavior and explore it a little further. Allow yourself to look beyond the behavior to see what might live underneath it. For instance, some people don't honor their commitments or they show up late because they have a deep-seated need to be in control. In other cases, people don't value their own commitment to themselves and therefore it's reflected in the way they treat others.

Upon recognizing the behavior, where it comes from, and why it's happening, you can take the next step. Try something new. Make a plan that you know you will keep. See it through as an exercise in creating a new pattern. Sometimes the best way to clean up an old pattern is to understand where it came from and then consciously choose to do things differently.

Miracle Message #59:

Honor your commitments.
Show up for yourself and the world.

#MiraclesNow

#60: CELEBRATE YOUR SMALL SUCCESSES.

Most people (including me) spend a lot of time focusing on what we do wrong. Whether we realize it or not, we can spend hours putting ourselves down. These thoughts range from *Why did you do that again?* to *You're not good enough* and *Who are you to be great?* Maybe you feel a low-level sense of insecurity, but you can't quite put your finger on where it comes from or how it affects you. Or maybe you feel upset but don't know why.

It seems we've become accustomed to focusing on the negative, looking for fault in all situations. I noticed this pattern while working with a private coaching client. Each time we'd have a session, she'd berate herself for all the things she perceived she'd done wrong. She'd list all her mistakes and nonchalantly put herself down. Then, during one coaching session, I suggested she start talking about what she did right. Confused, she responded, "But why?" I said, "You spend so much time focusing on what you did wrong. What if you chose to focus on what you do right?" She took a deep breath and mustered up the courage to begin listing her accomplishments.

After a few minutes of her focusing on the good stuff, I heard the tone of her voice change and noticed her energy shift. By redirecting her focus off what was wrong and onto what was right, she changed her entire attitude.

Though this exercise may seem simple, it's not an obvious choice. Our ego has convinced us that it's safe to focus on the negative and that we need to dwell in that space in order to be productive, move forward, or get by. In reality, the opposite is true. The moment we begin to celebrate ourselves and focus on our successes is the moment we begin living. So it's time to celebrate! Bust out your notebook and make a list of all the ways you rock. Don't be shy. Don't even be humble. Brag! Then take this list with you throughout the day and reference it whenever you're in doubt. As you notice great things about yourself throughout the day, add to the list. Continue to expand upon the list and enjoy the process.

Let this become an involuntary practice—so that eventually you no longer need the written list but instead start to take mental notes of how great you are. This exercise is about making the celebration of YOU a new habit. Not only will it feel great to focus on the good stuff, it will help you slowly but surely disconnect from your attachment to the bad stuff. Let the YOU party begin.

Miracle Message #60:

The moment we begin to celebrate ourselves and focus on our successes is the moment we begin living.

#MiraclesNow

#61: TO KEEP THE PEACE, KEEP IT REAL.

My friend Rachel has the hardest time disappointing people. She avoids conflict at all cost, going to great lengths to accommodate others. In most cases she will not tell the truth about what she needs, wants, and feels so that other people don't get upset. This behavior always leaves Rachel feeling drained, disappointed, and unconsciously resentful of herself and others. Worst of all, whenever Rachel doesn't speak her truth, she feels like a victim, yet she can't see how she created the dynamic in the first place.

I've been in this situation many times in the past. Whenever I don't speak my truth or ask for what I want in an effort to avoid conflict, I walk away resentful. Are you ever like Rachel? When faced with conflict, do you do everything in your power to smooth things over, even at the risk of your own happiness? If so, it's important to understand the pattern and use this exercise to change your behavior. People-pleasing to avoid conflict doesn't help you or the other party involved. Learn to rise up with your truth and take responsibility for your own needs. Conflict will occur from time to time; when it does, here's how to handle it with grace.

Step 1: See your part. It's likely that when you avoid conflict, you walk away feeling victimized in some way. You probably don't realize that your avoidance created the situation. It's crucial that you look honestly at how you avoid conflict and take responsibility for the outcome of the situation. Owning your part will help you release your resentment toward the other person and prepare you to take care of your own side of the street.

Step 2: Speak your truth. Once you're crystal clear about how you avoid conflict, it's time to change your pattern. Immediately get into the practice of speaking your truth. As awkward as it may feel, do your best to be forthright and honest about what you need and want. You can be mindful about the other person's feelings without denying your own. This is a delicate balance between being totally truthful and profoundly kind. When the truth is delivered with kindness it will be well received.

When my friend Rachel began to apply these tools to her relationships, she realized that her kind truth was actually welcomed. People appreciated her honesty, and because it was delivered in a kind tone she received a kind response.

Your truth is the kinder choice.

Miracle Message #61:

If you want to keep the peace, keep it real.

#MiraclesNow

#62: TAKE A ONE-MINUTE GRATITUDE BREAK

When we're busy or overwhelmed, it's easy to lose track of what matters. When life is hectic, we tend to focus on lack: what we don't have, what isn't working, and so on. Over time, focusing on the negative can stress us out. Whenever I'm in this place I call my dear friend Terri Cole, who is a licensed psychotherapist and a rock star life coach. Terri always knows how to calm my crazy.

A great tool that Terri suggests is the one-minute gratitude break. She says:

> If you are feeling stressed, anxious, or fearful, keep pictures of beautiful landscapes, loved ones, or any images that inspire you on your phone or computer screen. Take a solid 60 seconds to look at the pictures and conjure the feeling of gratitude and joy in the center of your chest. Focus on inhaling for a slow count of five and exhaling for a slow count of five. Come back to the present moment and feel gratitude for all that is right in your life right now.

I love this exercise, and it works every time! When we focus on negative thoughts, we lower our energy and block our capacity to be happy, healthy, and vital. But if we focus on the good stuff, we increase our energy in every area of our lives. When we redirect our attention onto something soothing and joyful, we focus on what we do have rather than what we think we don't. We can easily reenergize by shifting our focus onto something that makes us feel good.

This tool can be used anywhere, anytime. Keep an image in your wallet that will help you ignite the feeling of joy. Whenever you catch yourself going to Crazy Town, just open your wallet and reach for the image of inspiration. Take one minute to fully feel the feeling that comes over you when you look at this image. The more you practice this principle, the more empowered you will feel. Our ability to change our minds is one of our greatest tools for achieving peace.

Miracle Message #62:

Our ability to change our minds is
one of our greatest tools for achieving peace.

#MiraclesNow

#63: SOMETIMES NO IS THE MOST LOVING RESPONSE.

For many years I was a YES-er. I'd say yes to everyone, often overextending myself to the point of burnout. Saying yes all the time led to a lot of turmoil in relationships, work, and friendships.

In retrospect I can see how this behavior stemmed from a deep-rooted desire to be liked and approved of. Somewhere deep down I thought that saying yes meant that I was going to gain friends and seem cool and easygoing.

As time went on I came to realize that "yes" was not always the most loving response. I learned that saying no to what I didn't want to do or what I couldn't actually commit to would always wind up being the best decision. In time, "no" became a big part of my vocabulary. As a result of saying no more often, I had more time to focus on myself and I could actually show up for the commitments I had made. The word "no" saved me from a lot of meltdowns.

Are you a YES-er? If so, it's likely that you feel overwhelmed by all that you've agreed to do. One of the greatest ways to be productive, fulfilled, and less stressed out is to stop saying yes to everything and become more discerning about your commitments.

Some folks are uncomfortable saying no. If that's the case for you, begin simply saying this affirmation throughout the day: "It's safe to say no. When I say no I'm taking care of myself and others." This affirmation can guide you out of the underlying call to say yes, even when you know it's wrong.

As you begin to make the word "no" a greater part of your vocabulary, you'll come to feel a sense of peace set in. Though it may feel odd at first, you'll learn to love the freedom you'll receive from protecting your time and energy. Most important, you'll feel better about yourself because the things you do commit to you'll actually show up for.

Miracle Message #63:

Sometimes NO is the most loving response.

#MiraclesNow

#64: STILLNESS IS THE KEY TO SUCCESS.

At 25, I came to learn the blessing of stillness. In my case I had to hit an emotional, spiritual, and physical bottom in order to slow down. I guess it doesn't matter how I got there. All that matters is that I was finally still. Through meditation, prayer, and my commitment to an inner awareness, I was able to realize that my greatest accomplishments would come from stillness. This is when I really started living.

When we still our mind and body we can truly connect with our spirit. Once we establish a spiritual connection, our job is to follow the guidance we receive. Slowing down and listening is the key to living a guided life. In stillness we hear, and then it's our job to take Good Orderly Direction from a **God** of our own understanding.

I once heard the great entrepreneur and yogi Russell Simmons say, "I used to think anxiety and insomnia drove me to success, but it was the stillness that let me be good at anything. When you extend the seconds of stillness, that's when you're able to think and learn." Russell nailed it. Living a guided life is about extending the seconds of stillness. As we add up the moments of stillness we feel life begin to flow. What we need comes directly to us, life lessons are no longer so difficult, and we have a greater awareness of our purpose and our connection to the world. Stillness is where it's at.

Up to this point in the book you've received a lot of tools for achieving stillness and peace. Check in with yourself right now and ask, "Am I applying my tools?" If the answer is yes, take note as to how these tools have brought stillness and flow into your life. If the answer is no, ask yourself what you may be resisting. We are more than halfway through this process and it's time for a come-to-Jesus check-in. Get honest about your practice and know that it's never too late to recommit.

Let this principle be an exercise in shifting your focus from "out there" to "in here." Whenever you catch yourself back on that hamster wheel of anxiety, stress, and control, say: "Stillness is the key to my success."

Miracle Message #64:

Stillness is the key to success.

#MiraclesNow

#65: MEDITATE TO PREVENT FREAKING OUT.

Are you the type of person who needs to break down before you break through? For many years that was the case for me. Before I had Kundalini meditations and a greater connection to my energy, I had some epic freak-outs. Though I had many tools for managing my thoughts, I didn't have great guidance on how to bust through the really tough times and save myself from a freak-out.

One of the best ways to prevent a freak-out is to change your energy through your breath. Every 90 to 120 breaths the dominance changes from one nostril to another. A powerful way to shift your state of mind is to actively change the dominant nostril using this Kundalini meditation. In this exercise you're guided to notice which nostril is dominant when you're freaking out and then switch to the other nostril. When you switch the dominance from one nostril to the other you switch the dominance from one hemisphere of the brain to the other, which will enable you to look at things from a different perspective.

If you are irritated, angry, or in a funky state, practice this meditation. In just a few minutes you will be a different person.

Meditation to Prevent Freaking Out

Pose: Sit comfortably in Easy Pose with your spine straight.

Hands: Interlace your fingers with your right thumb on top. Place your hands at the center of your diaphragm, lightly touching your body. (As seen in the picture here.)

Eyes: Gently close your eyes.

Breath: Concentrate on your breath, bringing awareness to the tips of your nostrils. Notice which nostril is dominant right now. It may take a few moments to clarify the dominant nostril. Once you are aware of the dominant nostril, focus your attention on switching sides. Keep your shoulders down and relaxed. You can have pressure in your hands but none in your shoulders.

Continue changing the dominant nostril breath back and forth as long as you like.

Use this meditation whenever you need to prevent a freak-out. It's also a great one to teach young children.

This easy practice will be a powerful tool for them to carry into their future.

Miracle Message #65:

In the midst of a meltdown, breathe through the discomfort and you'll come out the other side.

#MiraclesNow

#66: "UNDERSTAND THROUGH COMPASSION OR YOU WILL MISUNDERSTAND THE TIMES."

One of Yogi Bhajan's Five Sutras for the Aquarian Age is, "Understand through compassion or you will misunderstand the times." Compassion is easy when we see people suffering. But what about having compassion for people who have wronged us?

This is a tough task. It's not easy to have compassion for someone who has treated you poorly, abused you, or attacked you in any way. In some cases it seems impossible. Often when we're treated poorly, compassion is the last thing on our minds. But for the sake of your happiness and the sanity of the world we all must learn to lean on compassion in these chaotic times.

I know for myself that it's very easy to have compassion for people who are struggling. My heart opens wide for anyone in need. But the moment someone has wronged me, it's very hard to call on my compassion muscles to clear the negativity and restore me to peace. In those situations I want to attack back to "protect myself" from feeling hurt. But when I feel the urge to get revenge of any kind, I pray for compassion, turning to this prayer from *A Course in Miracles*: "I can replace my feelings of depression, anxiety or worry with peace." This gentle reminder opens the door for compassion to set in. Remember: Compassion isn't something we create; it's something we experience.

When we open up our hearts and surrender our resentments, true compassion can come forward.

I feel that Yogi Bhajan was guiding us to use compassion as our greatest resource during these fear-based times. His hope was that we could see ourselves in the other person and let compassion be the energy through which we navigate our relationships and actions. When more people lead from a place of compassion, there will no longer be room for war, hatred, or attack. There will be peace.

Miracle Message #66:

"Understand through compassion or you will misunderstand the times." — Yogi Bhajan

#YogiBhajan #MiraclesNow

#67: "PROMOTE WHAT YOU LOVE INSTEAD OF BASHING WHAT YOU HATE."

One afternoon I was scrolling through my Twitter feed and I noticed an awesome post from my friend Jordan Bach, a well-known blogger and champion for gays. Jordan's post said, "Promote what you love instead of bashing what you hate." I immediately retweeted the post. Jordan, like many others, has been the victim of online attack and ridicule. He has dedicated his life and career to spreading empowering messages to the gay community. Though his intentions as a blogger are backed with love, he still gets ridiculed for them online. This is very painful and upsetting, though it hasn't stopped him from spreading his message.

I believe that the best way to combat attack and negativity is to spread more love. Rather than be the victim of ridicule, choose to be a beacon of light. Gandhi described himself as a "spiritual soldier, a soldier of peace." Why can't we access our own inner Gandhi in the face of conflict? There is so much negativity in the world today and in order to balance the energy, we must tap into our own inner Gandhi and choose to be a soldier for peace.

Take responsibility for the impact that your energy and intentions have on the world. If you're someone who's quick to place judgment, leave nasty comments on the web, or go out of your way to put others down, then it's time to take a good look at how your energy is contributing to the world. You have the power to elevate yourself and others if you choose to. Choose wisely.

Let Jordan's message become our anthem. Imagine what would happen if everyone just promoted what they loved rather than bashed what they hated? The world would be a happy, jammin' place.

Make this commitment in your own life. And if you want to take it a step further, share the Miracle Message below with your social media community and commit to a new way of being.

Miracle Message #67:

Promote what you love instead of
bashing what you hate. — Jordan Bach

#MiraclesNow

#68: HANDLE THE RESISTERS.

Two years ago my friend Marie was diagnosed with stage 4 metastatic breast cancer. Since her diagnosis, she's chosen to integrate her health care using conventional and holistic forms of treatment. Many people in her life have not been supportive of her choice, which has made her more fearful about her decision. Though Marie believes she's on the right path, she can't help but be affected by the resisters in her life.

We all have our own kinds of resisters. Dealing with resisters can be tough, whether it's a family member who tries to persuade you not to follow your career passion or a friend who challenges your beliefs. I often find that people resist the resistance—but that only makes things worse.

The most important thing for you right now is that you believe in what you're doing. Your faith will greatly support your intentions. As you shape your idea, dream, or goal, it's crucial that you bolster your faith. As your faith in your dreams grows stronger there will be less and less resistance from others. There are a few key ways to protect your energy and stay committed to what you believe. Outlined below are three tips that will greatly serve you when others resist your path.

1. It's helpful to disengage from conversations with resisters and, when possible, don't mention what you're up to. If people ask you

about your plans, don't get into the details. Protect your energy and your faith at all costs.

2. There's power in silence. When you're incubating your dreams, try to keep them to yourself as you flesh them out, fine-tune the details, and breathe life into them.

3. Only share when you're in full faith. If you have any fear surrounding your beliefs, be sure to clean it up before you share about it. Other people will reflect your own inner resistance. The moment you feel energetically committed to your decision, that's when you know you can share it. When you fully believe in what you're doing then others will reflect that faith back to you.

Miracle Message #68:

Honor your dreams and they will be honored.

#MiraclesNow

#69: HAVE IT ALL.

I had the privilege of attending a women's conference hosted by Arianna Huffington, at which I was surrounded by some of the most successful women in our country. Each panel discussion included CEOs, prominent news anchors, film directors, reporters, and more—all of whom were also mothers. Each woman openly discussed how hard it was to balance a successful career and a home life. They were all managing to keep it together, but much like any person who has a busy life, they were stressed.

Though there was an honest discussion of stress, each panelist shared plenty of empowering guidance. One theme that came up throughout the event was the fact that you can indeed "have it all," just not all at the same time. This idea resonated with me deeply. I have always wondered how one person can possibly manage "it all." Here was the answer! This message gave me hope. It helped me realize that, at different times in my life, I could focus my attention on what was important at that time rather than trying to be everything all at once.

If you are someone who gets overwhelmed by the idea that you need to "have it all," this principle is for you. Some of you may not resonate with this concept at first. In fact, I got some pushback on this principle when I posted it on my Facebook page. Some people stated that they believed that the Universe was abundant and that they deserved to have it all, and NOW! Though I agree that the Universe is abundant and conspiring to serve us at all times, there is a lot to be said for timing. I believe that the Universe is always working on our behalf—but I don't believe that it's always working in our time. It's important that we, as people on a spiritual path, accept that the Universe has a plan far greater than we do. So if we're guided to focus on different strengths at different times, then we must go with the flow rather than thrash against the current. When we flow toward what is working, rather than push into what isn't, we allow the Universe to lead us toward that which serves our highest good.

Miracle Message #69:

You can indeed have it all—just
not all at the same time.

#MiraclesNow

#70: FIND SPIRITUAL RUNNING BUDDIES.

Growing up I felt misunderstood. I had a hippie mom who took me along with her on the spiritual path; while we visited ashrams, my classmates went to the movies. As you can imagine, this didn't make much sense to my adolescent contemporaries. I often felt alone and a bit weird for following such a nontraditional path.

But in my midtwenties, when I fully surrendered to my own spiritual practice, I noticed that I was far from alone. I quickly attracted a powerhouse group of spiritual "running buddies," all of whom remain my best friends to this day. This ever-expanding group consists of people who walk their talk, share core beliefs, and support one another's growth. As I've deepened my spiritual practice, these spiritual running buddies have been by my side through the uncomfortable growth spurts and the breakthrough moments. I can't imagine a life without this spiritual posse.

In my workshops and lectures, I often hear people say that they feel alone on their spiritual paths. I tell them that their sense of isolation is a perception they have chosen. Our ego loves to convince us that we're separate, special, and alone. These folks often say things like, "No one understands me." Or, "My family and friends are not on the same page as me." What these people long for most is a spiritual running buddy.

If you're reading this book, it's likely that you're on a path of new discoveries and you've opened your heart and mind to a new perception. Embarking on that journey can feel lonely if you choose for it to be. "Choice" is the operative word. In this moment you can choose to attract more like-minded friends rather than choose to perceive yourself as separate. These days the spiritual choir has grown louder and louder. So the principle here is to trust that there is a power posse out there for you, too.

To attract a spiritual running buddy into your own life, follow three steps:

1. First, change your perception. If you've been walking around complaining that no one understands you, then you're not going to attract someone who does. Change the conversation and say that you are ready to connect with like-minded people.

2. Next, begin to pray for your spiritual running buddies to be guided to you. Trust that they are waiting for you, too, and that as soon as you clear space to meet them, they will hear your call. In this moment right now, you can say the prayer, "I welcome my spiritual running buddies into my life."

3. Finally, don't be afraid to make connections online. If you're a woman reading this, you can visit my social networking site and digital sisterhood, HerFuture.com. Or visit my Facebook fan page. I often hear that people meet on HerFuture or my fan page and stay spiritual running buddies forever.

Online relationships can be equally as strong.

Find your spiritual community. Open your mind, spirit, and social media stream to receive a spiritual running buddy of your own.

Miracle Message #70:

To grow further on my path of personal growth, I call on my spiritual running buddies for help.

#MiraclesNow

#71: REST, RELAX, RESTORE.

Millions of people suffer from insomnia or interrupted sleep. At some point we've all experienced what it's like to have a sleepless night. About 60 percent of people in the United States don't get enough sleep!

In technique #10 we discussed how sleep is a spiritual practice. At this point in your practice you know that sleep is crucial to your health. When you don't get enough sleep your body increases stress hormone levels and blood pressure, which can lead to heart disease, obesity, and depression. Herbert Benson's *The Relaxation Response* taught us that if we don't let our body rest, then it can't naturally heal itself. Sleep is the time when the body has a chance to repair. When your body can't repair itself, you not only feel ill but you also feel blocked. Your energy field is weakened, which diminishes your power presence. To realign your energy, vitality, and health, I've outlined a powerful Kundalini practice that will help restore your sleep patterns.

Yoga Nidra, or yogic sleep, is a deeply relaxing meditative practice that rejuvenates the body and mind. It's designed to balance the sympathetic and parasympathetic nervous systems, release physical tension, relax brain-wave activity, and balance the left and right sides of the brain. Yoga Nidra is often referred to as "sleep with awareness" because you can go into a space of deep relaxation without falling asleep.

To achieve this experience, you will follow my guided meditation, which will help you stay aware and present while relaxing your body. Be the witness of how your mind wanders and then gently and lovingly guide it back to the meditation.

Begin your practice lying comfortably on your back. You can cover yourself with a blanket if you're cold. Download my Yoga Nidra meditation at Gabbyb.tv /Miracles-Now. Listen to the meditation and do your best to stay awake while relaxing your entire body. As you listen to my guidance, identify each body part and stay present during this exercise. You can also read the directions below to guide yourself, or invite a friend to guide you. Practice Yoga Nidra for 1 to 11 minutes.

Lie flat on your back, with your arms stretched out by your sides, palms up (or whatever feels most comfortable).

Close your eyes.

Form a clear intention.

Take a couple of deep breaths, emphasizing exhalation.

Starting with your right side, rotate your awareness through all parts of the body, limb by limb, in fairly quick succession.

Become aware of each finger, palm of the hand, back of the hand, the hand as a whole, forearm, elbow, upper arm, shoulder joint, shoulder, neck, each section of the face (forehead, eyes, nose, chin, and so on), ear, scalp, throat, chest, side of the rib cage, shoulder blade, waist, stomach, lower abdomen, genitals, buttocks, whole spine, thigh, top and back of knee, shin, calf, ankle, top of foot, heel, sole, each toe.

Be aware of your body as a whole.

Repeat the rotation one or more times until adequate depth of relaxation is achieved, always ending with whole-body awareness.

Be aware of the whole body and the space surrounding it.

Feel the stillness and peace.

Reaffirm your initial intention.

Mentally prepare to return to ordinary consciousness.

To come out of Yoga Nidra, gently move your fingers for a few moments, take a deep breath, and then open your eyes.

Practicing Yoga Nidra may feel like you're taking a long nap, but you're still awake! You're rested but you're not asleep and dreaming. Instead, you are able to quiet your mind and come to a very blissful place.

Use this practice of Yoga Nidra whenever you feel sleep deprived. When I'm on a busy book tour or traveling throughout the country, this practice gets me through.

Miracle Message #71:

Sleep with awareness to relax and restore.

#MiraclesNow

#72: LET THE UNIVERSE DO HER THING.

My private coaching client Becky loves to control every detail of her life. The majority of her anxiety comes from her need to control outcomes. If she's on a date, she's focused on what will happen after dinner. If she achieves a goal, she immediately shifts her focus to what she needs to accomplish next. This behavior blocks her from truly experiencing her life and enjoying what she has in the present moment.

During one of our sessions, I suggested to Becky that she practice spending one day in full surrender. My suggestion was that each time she began to future-trip, she take a deep, full breath and say, "I let this go and allow the Universe to do her thing." The breath is a key component of making this principle work. An affirmation can change your mood, but a breath can change your life. Combining this surrender affirmation with a deep, full breath can bring you back into the present moment in an instant.

Though Becky resisted the exercise at first, she began to experience moments of peace. It helped her take in each moment (even if the moment truly lasted no longer than a second or two). In that instant she could release her need to future-trip and just let go. The more she proactively followed this practice, the more relaxed she became. In time she felt a deeper connection to the energy around her and she enjoyed the present knowing that the Universe was taking care of the future.

Future-tripping blocks us all in some way. Whenever we focus on what's coming next, we miss out on what's happening now. The next time you catch yourself tangled up in a future-trip, take a NOW vacation with your deep, full breath and the affirmation: *I let this go and allow the Universe to do her thing.* Pay close attention to how you feel after using this affirmation and enjoy the miraculous guidance you will receive.

Miracle Message #72:

I let go and allow the Universe to do her thing.

#MiraclesNow

#73: GIVE YOUR BRAIN A BREAK.

The concept of slowing down often seems alluring—but it can also be hard to do. Why? Simple. These days, everything moves so fast. Don't get me wrong—living a fast-paced life isn't a bad thing (and it's somewhat unavoidable in a place like New York City). But running on high speed all the time can make you feel overwhelmed. You not only end up getting less done, you feel tense and anxious.

Paradoxically, the secret to getting more done is simply to slow down. I'm not saying you should renounce the world and meditate all day. But I am suggesting that you clear space to access your inner power. When you do that, time will seem to expand, and you'll accomplish more. This principle will redirect your energy and help you heighten an inner sense of power to let your outer life grow, expand, and flow.

When there's a lot on your mind, it's hard to feel productive and at peace. My friend Michael Eisen taught me that a great way to enhance your energy and create more time in your day is to take regular brain breaks: mindful moments that let you clear your thoughts. Just step away from the computer and take a walk (and *don't* bring your phone). These breaks will allow you to mentally shake it all off and gain a fresh start when you get back to your daily routine.

Miracle Message #73:
When you're stressed out, take a brain break.
#MiraclesNow

#74: STOP BEING SO
DAMN NEGATIVE.

Every week I send out a video blog in my e-mail news-
letter. In the videos I riff on spiritual topics and offer up
advice. One week I sent out a video called "How to Handle
Negative People." Within minutes I received an e-mail
reply from a woman named Kimberly. She said, "Gabby, I
need you to blog—HOW TO STOP BEING NEGATIVE!
I have been told by many people that I am a negative person. I don't want to be this way anymore! What can I do?!"
Kimberly's request for help not only inspired me to do a
video about the topic, it prompted me to share the solution in this book. Being negative lowers your energy and
inhibits genuine connection with others. Turning your
low-vibe attitude upside down takes commitment, but it's
mandatory if you want to live a miraculous life.

In Kimberly's case, she reached the point where she
no longer wanted to be identified (by others or herself)
as "the negative person." She was ready for a new story.
The good news for her is that the story can be rewritten
anytime. It's never too late to drop the low-vibe BADitude
and start fresh.

The process of changing your attitude is both conscious and subconscious. Consciously, we must recognize the issue and surrender it. Subconsciously, we must
allow a spiritual transformation to take place. From the
perspective of *A Course in Miracles*, when we have the

wrong-minded (fear-based) perception of something, our job is to turn it over to the Holy Spirit (a.k.a. inner guide) to reinterpret it for us. When we surrender our fear-based choices to the care of our inner guide, we can let go and allow spirit to do her thing. The *Course* says, "Love will immediately enter into any mind that truly wants it." Therefore, by surrendering your negativity to your inner guide, you're saying that you *want* love instead.

Whenever you notice yourself stuck in the negative story, pray your way out. Begin by praying for a new perception. In those moments when you feel caught in the spiral of negativity, invite your inner guide to step in and reinterpret your inner dialogue for you. Then expect that your desire to see love instead is all you need to begin the path of new perceptions. You may start to feel a loving sensation come over you. Or you may find that you avoid conflict that day. Whatever the outcome, trust this process to take you out of your negative pattern and into a whole new way of being.

Miracle Message #74:

Surrender your low-vibe BADitude
to the care of your inner guide. Expect miracles.

#MiraclesNow

#75: UNBLOCK YOUR BOWELS, UNBLOCK YOUR LIFE.

I believe that the flow of our bowels has a direct correlation with the flow of our lives. Skeptical? Ask yourself if when you're feeling super stopped up, your life is stopped up, too. If you want to unblock every area of your life, you have to address *every* area!

It's important to recognize that your physical well-being directly affects your energy field—and that your energy is your true power. So let's focus on how your bowel movements can support the flow of your life.

Digestive issues often stem from our negative thoughts and anxiety. When we're anxious (for whatever reason) during meals, we're likely to chew our food quickly and incompletely, which makes it hard to digest. And if we're judging ourselves for what we're eating, then we're infusing negativity into the meal. When we put negative vibes into our food, we struggle to digest it. Our body tenses up and we get blocked.

A powerful tool I learned from one of my Kundalini friends is to bless your food before you eat it. My teacher suggested that I look at my food and say, "I love my food; my food loves me." This simple action can change your entire dining experience. You'll experience the richness of the flavors, you'll eat more slowly and deliberately, you won't overeat, and most important, you'll digest properly.

Taking a moment to bless your food can transform your eating patterns altogether.

Use this exercise to unblock your mind, unblock your bowels, and unblock your life.

Miracle Message #75:

I love my food; my food loves me.

#MiraclesNow

#76: RELEASE YOUR ENERGETIC HEADLOCK.

In relationships we often lose track of how our energy affects the other person. This is particularly true when we feel attached to the person. In some cases our over-powering energy—that unconscious energetic strangle-hold we have on the other person—can ruin relationships or sabotage opportunities. The early stages of a romantic relationship are especially susceptible, since you may be unclear about how the other person feels about you. The energetic headlock can also choke a work relationship; consider times when you've really wanted a boss to approve of you or a colleague to get something done. Whenever we feel attached or needy in a relationship, it's likely we have the other person in an energetic headlock.

As you probably know by now, holding someone in an energetic headlock won't get you very far. Typically that type of needy energy is a big turnoff. Let's face it: Who wants to date someone who's smothering them with their vibes? Or who wants to hire someone who's trying to manipulate an outcome?

This lesson isn't easy for people. Many folks have deep-rooted fearful beliefs such as, "I'm unworthy unless I have the attention of others." Or, "I need to control the outcome in order to feel safe." These beliefs stem from our upbringing, old traumatic experiences, and a deep need to feel safe and loved. Understanding the depth of these beliefs is crucial to changing your behavior.

Take a moment to identify and write down the fear behind your need to control others. For me it was, *I'm incomplete without a romantic partner.* That thought made me very controlling, manipulative, and energetically crazy in romantic relationships. My ego had convinced me that I was unsafe without a partner and therefore I needed to do whatever it took to keep a romantic relationship intact. When I realized the controlling behavior stemmed from one tiny mad idea, I was able to surrender it.

Once you have a greater understanding as to why you feel the need to control people energetically, you can move onto the next step: getting clear about the feeling behind the need to control. Is there a sensation of panic? A feeling of loss? Tension in some specific area of your body? Take a moment to describe the feeling. Give the feeling a color and a texture. Be as descriptive as possible. The feeling you're describing is the old insecurity and fear that lives underneath your need to control. That feeling was never healed, so you think you need to control the outside world to avoid ever feeling it again.

The key to releasing your need to energetically control others is to heal the feeling behind the need to control. Whenever you notice your stress levels rise and fear set in with the need to clamp down an energetic headlock, that's the moment to *feel* the feeling. Take 60 seconds to just breathe into the feeling, wherever it lives in your body. Maybe it's tightness in your stomach, a flutter in your chest, or a clenched jaw. Direct your breath to that area as you let yourself safely feel the feeling. In that minute your energy can shift, you can breathe through the feeling, and you can let go. The miracle of letting go comes when you get to the root of the problem. The goal isn't to get your desired outcome—the goal is peace.

Use this exercise whenever you're energetically out of control. Identify the feeling, breathe into it, and let it go. Continue this practice until it becomes second nature.

Miracle Message #76:

Obsessing over the outcome of a
relationship gets in the way. Let go and allow.

#MiraclesNow

#77: HARNESS THE POWER OF EMPATHY.

Many of us who are drawn to this type of book are considered empaths, otherwise referred to as "sensitive people." An empath has the ability to sense the energy of the people around them. Some of the prominent traits of an empath are an ability to detect deep emotions in others and a strong sense of knowing. These characteristics can be very powerful if they are fine-tuned. But when empaths are unaware of their heightened levels of intuition and empathy, the qualities can become overwhelming and sometimes scary.

Everything has an energetic vibration or frequency. As the vibrations change, empaths can experience the shift with their senses. Armed with the right tools, an empath can shift vibrations in a positive direction. It's important to have a heightened sense of awareness of your empathy so that you can ride the wave of the world's emotions rather than be taken down by those emotions. If you identify as an empath or even have the tendency to be affected by the energy of negative words, news, and people, this principle will greatly support you.

How can you use this trait for healing rather than harm? First, it's important to understand how negative vibrations affect you. Make a list of all the circumstances that lower your energy. Who's involved and what happens? Then make a commitment to protect yourself in those situations.

There are a few great techniques for protecting your energy. You can start with a prayer. I use this fabulous energy protection prayer I learned from my spiritual mentors in Brazil. Speak to God, the Universe, spirit, or whomever you talk to when you pray. Say out loud or to yourself: *Thank you for removing any negative energy I may have picked up, and thank you for retrieving any positive energy that I have lost.* This statement sends out the Universal message that your energy won't be messed with. You have more power than you think, so remember that you can call the shots when it comes to the type of energy you are willing to pick up.

Another great exercise is to shield yourself by envisioning a circle of light around you. Close your eyes and hold the vision of a beautiful shield of white light surrounding you. If you're in a space with toxic energy or you're picking up low vibes from the TV or radio, use the shield to protect your energy field.

As an empath, once you know how to protect yourself, you can learn how to use your abilities in a positive way. Empaths are often problem solvers. Their heightened levels of intuition help them bring solutions to situations that may seem hopeless. Use this skill to help yourself and others find peace in nonpeaceful situations and be a powerful empathetic source in the world.

Miracle Message #77:

Empathy is a virtue. Use it wisely.

#MiraclesNow

#78: DEAL WITH YOUR OWN MIND.

Yogi Bhajan said, "If your mind can go along with you, it is a blessing. If your mind obeys you, it is a super-blessing." The blessing is that when you learn to control your mind you're no longer controlled by it. You can lead the way with your higher self rather than with the low-level guidance of your ego. When you master your mind, you can experience what is called *shuniya* in the yogic tradition.

Shuniya (*shoo-nee-yuh*) is a state of awareness in which the mind is brought to complete stillness. When you develop this inner peace, you'll be rewarded with physical, emotional, and spiritual benefits. Yogi Bhajan called shuniya the most elevated state of consciousness, in which the ego is brought to complete stillness. Power exists in that stillness. When we experience "zero mind" we can focus our mental projection on clear intentions and align with the power source of the universe.

Does this all sound a little trippy? I know the concept of "zero mind" might seem hard to grasp, but it's fully achievable. You can reach stillness with a meditation called Dealing with Your Own Mind. You can receive great benefits from this meditation in minutes. If you still your mind even for an instant, you're one step closer to experiencing shuniya. Use this practice to achieve moments of stillness or expand your inner awareness. Make it a daily ritual.

To begin the practice, sit in Easy Pose with your spine straight. Close off your right nostril with your right thumb and inhale deeply through your left nostril. Exhale completely through your mouth.

Practice this meditation for six minutes.

To close the meditation, inhale deeply; interlace your fingers and stretch them over your head with your palms up. Hold your breath for 10 to 15 seconds while you stretch your spine upward.

Miracle Message #78:

Mastering your mind helps unlock the mystery of existence.

#MiraclesNow

#79: GET A NATURAL LOVE RUSH.

Sometimes the simplest way to drop the BADitude and bring on the happiness can come through an everyday action. Certain actions activate oxytocin, otherwise called the love hormone because it's known to induce feelings of love and trust, and a sense of bonding. When you're feeling funky, oxytocin can turn your mood around, make you feel more connected, and revive your overall energy.

There are a few natural ways to rev up the oxytocin engine when your energy is sputtering. These great tips can be applied anywhere, anytime. Take a minute for a miracle and let the love hormone lead the way.

Tip 1: Place your hand on your heart. My friend Arielle Ford taught me that by putting your own hand on your heart you stimulate the love hormone, which sends your body the signal that it's safe to calm down. Once you've placed your hand onto your heart, breathe into it. As you breathe into your heart imagine feelings of love, compassion, and ease passing over you. Proactively collaborate in your healing by breathing into your heart.

This exercise will stimulate the flow of oxytocin. Stress will subside as oxytocin helps lower blood pressure and cortisol (read: stress) levels. The anxiety-busting effects support growth, healing, and overall happiness. Place your hand on your heart and calm down the crazy.

Tip 2: Give someone a 20-second hug. Yup, it's that simple. Just give someone you love a little squeeze, and let it linger. Make sure the hug is reciprocated. It's important that the gesture ignite a sense of connection to stimulate oxytocin. Hug your lover, your best friend, or even your pet. The sweet connection between two beings can totally change your mood.

Tip 3: Flaunt your pearly whites. A genuine, heartfelt smile creates a sense of connection. Smile at people you know, and feel free to smile at random folks you pass on the sidewalk. Just express authentic, heart-centered grace through the generous gesture of a smile. In an instant you'll feel love rush in.

Love doesn't have to come from a romantic partner or a family member. Love can come from any form of authentic connection. Take time in your life to create those connections and trust that you're not serving yourself alone; you're also spreading the love.

Miracle Message #79:

Love can come from any form
of authentic connection.

#MiraclesNow

#80: THE QUALITIES WE DISLIKE IN OTHERS ARE DISOWNED PARTS OF OUR SHADOW.

I once had a blow-out fight with a woman working at a car rental counter. She flaunted her power and went out of her way to make things difficult for me. My reaction wasn't so cute. I felt the need to respond with my own power play by threatening to call her manager and make a complaint. And I did just that.

Hours after stating my claim to her corporate office and regional manager, I felt no better. I thought that complaining about how poorly I was treated would help me get over the experience. Oddly, it made me feel worse. I sat with the feeling and explored what the lesson was for me. In stillness I heard my inner voice say, *The qualities you don't like in this person are a disowned part of your own shadow.* I was floored by my inner guide: The message was so clear and resonant.

I went on to examine what it was about this angry rental agent that reflected my "disowned shadow." What was it in me that was being hidden and suppressed? In silent contemplation, I was able to accept that deep down there was a part of me that wanted to control the situation and the outcome. This was the same quality she'd displayed. Her deep-rooted need to be in control came head to head with my need to be in control, and all hell broke loose.

The key point here is that even complete strangers can offer us opportunities to look closer at the shadow sides of ourselves that we want to keep hidden. *A Course in Miracles* teaches, "The *hidden* can terrify not for what it is, but for its hiddenness." The issue isn't what we're hiding, it's that we're unwilling to address it.

The next time someone riles you up, witness your reaction and remember that *the qualities you don't like in them are a disowned part of your shadow.* Be still and allow your inner guide to teach you what it is that you need to release. Be willing to look more closely at your ego and let the people of the world be your greatest teachers.

Miracle Message #80:

The qualities we don't like in others are a disowned part of our shadow.

#MiraclesNow

#81: MAKE DECISIONS WITH EASE.

Often our logical mind gets in the way of our clear intuition. When a situation has a lot of variables (or the stakes seem high), all the back-and-forth and inner debating can make us crazy. Many of us have a tendency to overanalyze, too, which makes it all worse by cutting off our connection to inspiration and intuition. When we're mired in indecision, we'll often force an answer. But pressuring ourselves into a decision is usually a recipe for regret. The ideal way to make decisions is from a place of intuition and power.

Every muscle in your body either resists a decision or flows with it. Your brain might play tricks on you, but your muscles never lie. When you feel stuck about a decision, you can test your options against your muscle tension to see which direction your body actually agrees with. This is called applied kinesiology testing and it is a way to get answers from your subconscious through muscle reactions.

Here's a simple muscle test that you can do right now.

Begin by selecting your question. A question can be as small as "Should I eat this pizza?" or as big as "Is it time to leave my job?"

Once you've decided on your question, rephrase it as though you've decided on it ("Yes, I want the slice of pizza"; "No, I'm not ready to leave my job").

Press the tips of your left thumb and little finger together so they form a sort of O (as seen in the picture).

Insert the top sections of thumb and index finger of your right hand into the opening (as seen below).

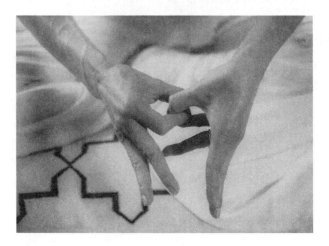

Then pull your right thumb and index finger against the fingers of your left hand that are forming the O.

If the O separates easily, it means this choice makes you weak and your body doesn't support it. This is a clear indication that your answer is a definite NO.

If your left fingers stay tight together, the choice you're making is a strong YES.

This simple exercise can communicate so much. Trust that your muscles never lie. Your ego may resist the messages you receive, but do your best to trust what your body is telling you.

Miracle Message #81:

Make decisions from a place of intuition and power.

#MiraclesNow

#82: DON'T DANCE AROUND THE PERIMETER OF WHO YOU WANT TO BE. DIVE IN FULLY.

When I was 25, I became a devotee of the spiritual teacher Marianne Williamson. One of her books in particular hit me straight in the heart: *A Woman's Worth*. After reading it, I was awakened to a power source within me I had never recognized before. This awesome awakening occurred upon reading the following passage:

> A queen is wise. She has earned her serenity, not having had it bestowed on her but having passed her tests. She has suffered and grown more beautiful because of it. She has proved she can hold her kingdom together. She has become its vision. She cares deeply about something bigger than herself. She rules with authentic power.

At the time, I couldn't comprehend what it would feel like to "rule with authentic power," but it sounded really groovy. I wanted to perceive myself as a powerful woman, but deep down I felt like a weak girl seeking my self-worth from outside circumstances. This passage helped me recognize that there are no shortcuts on the path to my authentic power. I would have to show up for life's assignments and pass my tests to release all that was blocking me from being my highest self.

Once I became willing to stop looking *out there* and look inward instead, my entire life changed. I began to *earn my serenity* and learned to find my source of peace and purpose from an inward condition. My neediness melted away, my insecurity lessened, and my self-doubt transformed into self-assurance. In time I became a queen, and today I live in my authentic power. You, too, have the capacity to live in your authentic power. If you feel out of alignment in any area of your life, use my tools below to recalibrate your authenticity.

Take out your pen and paper and describe the differences between what it feels like to be in your truth versus what it feels like to be in your ego. How do you act differently, talk differently, think, and even breathe differently? Pay close attention to the differences in how you feel. Be as specific as you can be—no action, habit, or word is too small to notice.

Though these steps seem subtle, you can trust that they are igniting transformational shifts within you. Stay committed to this process and invite the energy of the Universe to support your assignments and spiritual growth. Trust that your authentic power is all you need to truly share your light with the world.

Miracle Message #82:

Don't dance around the perimeter of the person you want to be. Step in fully and completely.

#MiraclesNow

#83: THE F IN FORGIVENESS IS FOR FREEDOM.

As a student of *A Course in Miracles,* I have become committed to practicing the F word, a.k.a. forgiveness. The *Course* emphasizes that through the experience of forgiveness we can reconnect with our truth, which is love. The disconnection from truth is what causes us so much pain in the first place. Whenever we choose to perceive the world through attack, judgment, and separation, we unconsciously feel guilty because deep down we know we've turned our backs on love. Forgiveness sets us free from guilt and realigns us with who we truly are.

The idea of forgiveness is great, but the actual experience of it may seem hard to do. Many people cannot fathom what it would be like to forgive because they've created a life in which they're constantly on the defensive, "protecting" themselves at all costs. If you're someone who keeps their boxing gloves up, it's time to drop the fighting stance. The only way to truly flourish in your life is to release all the tension that holds you back from letting love pour through you. That tension stems from a lack of forgiveness. Now, I truly understand that in many cases it may seem impossible to forgive a person or a situation, particularly if the act was deeply harmful to you. When you've been hurt it's normal to feel like you cannot let go of your anger and attack thoughts. You're convinced that in some way your anger will protect you, arm you, and keep you strong. But in reality, anger and resentment weaken you by keeping you stuck in past pain.

Forgiveness is crucial to your happiness. It's important to understand and accept that forgiveness is not for your attacker. It's for you. Through forgiveness you put down the boxing gloves and open your heart to peace.

Ready to experience miracles now? Follow these three steps to exercise forgiveness.

Step 1: In your journal, write a list of the people you need to forgive. (Don't forget to include yourself if necessary.)

Step 2: Acknowledge your part in the situation. Though you may feel that you've been deeply wronged, you, too, have a part. Sometimes your part may be that you've been carrying the resentment. Or maybe your part is that you stuck around in a relationship for too long. If it's not obvious what your part is, just take a moment to ask yourself how you've been participating in your own discomfort around the situation.

Step 3: Pray. Through prayer we ask an invisible teacher for help. Call it Holy Spirit, call it God, or call it love. The name doesn't matter. What matters is that you choose to call on it. Trusting that a power greater than you can intervene in the situation is a most crucial step in the forgiveness process. Your logical mind has no freakin' clue as to how you'll possibly forgive and let go. But your intuition and higher consciousness have the perfect plan. Trust in that plan and surrender to your desire to forgive through a prayer.

Simply say, "Inner guide, I recognize that this resentment is causing me harm. My anger and attachment are not serving me. I am willing to forgive. Show me the way. Thank you."

Feel free to change the language around this prayer. The words don't matter nearly as much as your intention to let go.

Miracle Message #83:

To truly flourish is to release all the tension that holds you back from letting love pour through you.

#MiraclesNow

#84: WHEN THE TIME IS ON YOU, START AND THE PRESSURE WILL BE OFF.

You may be familiar with the song "Age of Aquarius" from the musical *Hair*. The talk of this age became even more prevalent in 1969 when Yogi Bhajan moved to the States to share the hidden technology of Kundalini yoga. His intention in bringing Kundalini to the West was to prepare us for the Aquarian age. Well, the Aquarian Age is now officially here.

You may know from astronomy lessons that Earth rotates on an axis. The line going through the center of the planet has a slight wobble to it; when this axis is shifted, we move into a new age roughly, every 2,000 years. For the last 50 years we've been transitioning from the Piscean Age to the Aquarian Age. The Aquarian Age officially began on November 11, 2011, or 11/11/11. You may also hear the date December 21, 2012 as the official turning point. Regardless of the date you accept as the turning point, we are here now.

In the Aquarian Age we are experiencing a whole new dimension of human potential and spiritual awareness. With this shift also comes a sense of time speeding up. Many people express the feeling of being in a pressure cooker about to burst.

In an effort to prepare us for these tumultuous times, Yogi Bhajan left us with five sutras for the Aquarian Age (as referenced in earlier principles). The third sutra, "When the time is on you, start and the pressure will be off," offers us great guidance in how to navigate the pressure of this time. This message encourages us to ride the energy and take action now. We are no longer in an age in which we can hide out, play small, and stay stuck. If we do that, we'll feel great discomfort.

Often people resist change. They feel safer in the same place. The goal of this sutra is to help us accept that the Universe is change and change is constant. We must embrace change and flow with it. The moment you take the first step the pressure will be off.

Miracle Message #84:

"When the time is on you, start and the pressure will be off." — Yogi Bhajan

#YogiBajan #MiraclesNow

#85: INTIMATE RELATIONSHIPS CAN BE YOUR GREATEST LEARNING DEVICE.

Intimate relationships can often provide a revelatory path for personal growth. Perhaps in the heat of the moment when every button is pushed, it's hard to see the lesson. Whether it's your spouse, parent, child, or even a best friend, you may find it difficult to navigate the disagreements or tough patches. But often the relationships that have the most to offer us are the ones that bring up all our funky stuff.

If you show up for these relationships with no willingness to grow, then you'll be caught in a negative spiral. Our work as spiritual students is to accept that the intimate relationships in our lives are divine assignments for optimal growth and healing. When we perceive relationships in this way we can use them as learning devices rather than death sentences.

Yogi Bhajan said:

> Two polarities are joined together to pull life together through hard and even times. But nowadays we think of relationships as staying together through even times only. How can it be possible that through any relationship you cannot have hard and even times?

I love this message because it gives us permission to accept that we will have hard times. With acceptance comes truth and a desire to grow. Rather than expecting to live in peace all the time, our job is to be at peace with the chaos.

This principle is geared toward exercising your desire to find peace in emotionally charged relationships. I have found that my most intimate relationships mirror the parts of me that I just don't want to see. They push me to the edges of my comfort zone and they challenge me to grow. Here are some of the tools I suggest for clearing the challenges in emotionally charged relationships.

Acknowledge your desire to be right. The moment we accept that we'd rather be happy than right is the moment we are set free. In that decision, you can choose to be nonreactive. In the heat of the moment, instead of responding in your typical manner (which probably pisses off the other person and makes everything worse), don't do anything.

For instance, I used to get very defensive and reactive when faced with challenges in relationships. That reactive energy got me nowhere. I finally got so fed up with myself that I decided to change—to make a proactive decision rather than succumb to reactions. Instead of doing what I always did when a challenge arose, I chose to do nothing. I chose to breathe through the discomfort and be still. In that stillness, I could hear my intuition tell me how to navigate the rest of the fight in order to find peace more quickly. This exercise may cause alarm for the other person because they expect you to respond as you always do. Trust that your stillness will not only serve you, but it will also offer them an opportunity to shift, too.

Another powerful tool for shifting the energy of a super-charged relationship is to accept that the other person has a totally different perception of the world than you do. Sometimes the path of least resistance is to agree to disagree. The key here is to honor the other person's opinion even if it's the opposite of your own. We all have egos that perceive the world through fearful lenses. By honoring the fact that each person is having their own fearful experience, you give yourself permission to let go of your need to be right and you set each other free.

Use these tools for smoothing out the rough edges of your intimate relationships and trust that these are divine assignments for optimal growth and healing.

Miracle Message #85:

Let your intimate relationships be your greatest learning devices for spiritual growth and healing.
#MiraclesNow

#86: BE THE HAPPY LEARNER.

As we come closer to the end of *Miracles Now,* it's time to begin evaluating your daily practice. Though you've been given many tools, perhaps none of them have stuck yet. It's important to understand that you don't have to apply all these principles at once. Simply choosing one tool to practice daily can change your life forever. True change comes from daily repetition of new and empowering actions. These actions can be small and still have a massive benefit.

At this point, take an inventory of the exercises that have served you. Maybe choose one that can support you greatly at this time and make the commitment to apply it for the next 40 days. The repetition of that new behavior will help you create permanent change that will last a lifetime.

It's easy to get overwhelmed when you're given a ton of tools. Some people even become addicted to personal growth and then their egos get them down by saying they're not doing enough. I take the opposite approach. I believe in adding up subtle shifts. I also believe in repetition. There's no need to push, control, or force anything to happen. Trust that real change occurs subtly over time.

If you've been trying to control outcomes and force your spiritual path, it's time to surrender and become the happy learner. Trust that you don't need to do everything perfectly and you don't need to do it all right now. Just do one thing at a time and let the Universe be in charge.

As you continue with the techniques in this book, practice being imperfect, too. Take your time, revisit past exercises, and maybe even choose just one to focus on for 40 days. This book is not designed for you to do all at once. It's a self-study curriculum. Trust your intuition and let your inner voice lead you to the exercises that are best for you at this time.

Miracle Message #86:

Keep it simple. Go slow. Be the happy learner.

#MiraclesNow

#87: TRUST YOUR GUT.

Are you still having trouble making decisions even after practicing the kinesiology test from principle #81? Sometimes our egos can really get in the way of coming to an honest conclusion. We also can get hung up on other people's opinions. Though the muscle-testing exercise may have given you some clarity, it's possible that you need to learn to trust your intuitive muscles more fully.

This principle is designed for the serious skeptics who need a little extra *oomph* in their decision-making process. This exercise is utterly simple, yet it instantly reveals your true feelings on a matter. Bust it out when you're mired in frustration and totally unable to make a decision. After hours (or days or weeks) of hesitating and over-analyzing, this quick exercise brings you relief and lets you move forward.

Grab a coin from your wallet. Then think about the two choices you're mulling over. Name choice number one heads and choice number two tails. Then flip the coin. Immediately after the coin toss, ask yourself how you feel.

Are you happy and excited by the verdict—or are you anxious and frightened? What is your honest reaction to the outcome of your coin toss?

If you took this exercise seriously, it's likely you've gained some important insight about what you intuitively want or don't want. The moment the coin landed on heads or tails was a moment for you to honestly assess how you felt about the outcome. That honest response is your truth. It may surprise you. Sometimes we think we should want a certain outcome for whatever reason (it's easier, others want it, it seems more "like" us, and so on), so it's hard to admit that we actually want the other option. The coin flip lets you mentally step back from the decision and distance yourself from all the analytical chatter so that, ultimately, you can recognize your own instincts.

Use this tool whenever you're in doubt and you'll learn to trust your gut.

Miracle Message #87:

Trust that your gut reaction is the truth underneath the surface of your fears.

#MiraclesNow

#88: CHANGE YOUR MOOD WITH A RITUAL.

My friend Barbara Biziou is the queen of rituals. She has a ritual for everything! Barbara says, "Rituals give substance and meaning to our lives—enhancing daily routines, enriching milestones, and guiding us through difficult transitions." Each time I practice one of Barbara's rituals I feel reenergized, as though I've pressed the REFRESH button on my life.

There's one ritual in particular that I find beneficial: the ritual to shift your energy. This simple practice has the capacity to totally shift my energy and my mood in an instant.

Barbara's ritual for changing your energy goes like this:

Crush some black peppercorns in a bowl and smell them. Black pepper releases negativity and wards off bad vibes immediately, making more space in your aura (an aura is a field of luminous energy that surrounds a living creature). You can also use pure essential oil of black pepper. If you want extra courage, carry some in a bag—it helps you face things you need to and gives you the extra energy to do the things you just don't want to do.

With your eyes open, take a few deep breaths. Sit up and pull your shoulders back as you breathe from the top of the lungs. With your eyes up, take a few deep breaths of release. This puts you in a happy brain state.

Now close your eyes and lower your chin until you are sitting in a comfortable position. As you take a few deep breaths, imagine you can open to energy of peace and compassion. Imagine the energy flowing through you like warm soothing water, dissolving the harsh barriers that you have created to protect your inner light. Set your intention that only what is appropriate to be dissolved at this time will be released. It is your choice. It is like connecting or plugging in to a cosmic battery. Open and allow this force field to fill your entire being.

Now imagine that you have an invisible cloak around you. Only good and positive energy can enter and you now have the ability to safely share your true essence with the world. Seal this energy by burning lavender incense or dried lavender flowers, or by anointing yourself with pure lavender essential oil.

For the ritual newcomer, this may seem like witchcraft, but if you are fully committed to enhancing your energy, then take this seriously. Whenever you commit to practicing a ritual, you make a statement to the Universe that you're willing to shift, grow, and change. Trust me: That statement is being heard. Even if you're a cynic, test-drive this ritual and notice the miraculous shifts.

Miracle Message #88:

Rituals shift energy and make a
positive statement to the Universe.

#MiraclesNow

#89: MAKE MONEY AND MIRACLES.

In the wake of a national recession, financial fear and insecurity soar. While on the road for the *May Cause Miracles* book tour in 2013, I talked to so many people who felt strangled by their fear of not having enough. But even when the economy is sailing, we can feel trapped and panicked by our thought patterns around money. The only way through the fear is to shift your perception around your finances.

Energy is currency. When your energy has an essence of abundance, you greatly increase your capacity to receive more abundance. Yogi Bhajan said it best: "You run after wealth and glory and glamour. But it will run after you, providing you are an open channel." When you open up your channel to release financial fears, you'll come to accept that you are not your lack mentality. This practice will help you rev up your creative capacity to exchange and receive financial abundance.

Begin by honestly stating your financial fears. Say them firmly to yourself or out loud, or write them down. Once you've taken an inventory, the next step is to surrender them fully through a powerful prayer.

Abundance prayer

Thank you, Universe [or God], for helping me reinterpret my relationship to money. I know my lacking thoughts are based on fear and I'm ready to release them now. I welcome new and creative abundance and I will pay attention to the guidance I receive. I am free from financial fear.

Then sit in meditation and allow the miracle to set in. You can follow the guided meditation below or download the Abundance Meditation from Gabbyb.tv/Miracles-Now.

Abundance meditation

Take a deep breath in your nose and exhale out your mouth.

With each inhale, expand your diaphragm, and on the exhale, contract your diaphragm in and up. Deepen your breath with every inhale and exhale.

On the inhale, recite this mantra mentally: *I have enough.*

On the exhale, say: *I am being taken care of.*

Inhale: *I know there is enough to go around.*

Exhale: *I release my financial fear and welcome a miracle.*

Continue this mantra as you inhale and exhale. Let the words settle in and trust that you're being guided to new perceptions.

Miracle Message #89:

I welcome abundance and I will
pay attention to the guidance I receive.

#MiraclesNow

#90: "'NO' IS A COMPLETE SENTENCE."

My dear friend Latham Thomas, an author and inspirational speaker, has a simple yet profound saying that serves me well: "'No' is a complete sentence." Saying no can be tough at times, especially when you're afraid to disappoint someone.

Though I pride myself on being someone who has clear boundaries, I still find my way into some sticky situations in which I feel uncomfortable saying no. This came up recently when I was trying to work out a business deal with people I really like. We'd spent months on countless conference calls mulling over the deal points and ironing out the legalese. After all the effort, I felt obligated to move forward with the deal even though everything in my being was telling me not to. Logically and spiritually the deal just didn't seem right. My friend Marie Forleo's words rang in my ears: "If it's not a hell yes, it's a hell no."

Though I was super clear about my answer, I totally lost track of it when I got on another conference call with the team. While on the call, I noticed myself getting nervous and uncomfortable with the idea of letting everyone down. I started to go along with their plan and by the time we hung up the phone, I was still 100 percent committed—but I didn't want to be.

Why was it so hard to say no? After some reflection it became clear that I still have issues letting people down.

Because we'd spent so much time working out the deal, I felt a false sense of obligation.

To work through this discomfort, I sat on my meditation pillow and asked my inner guide to help me move forward. After a few minutes of stillness, I heard my friend Latham's voice in my mind saying, *"No" is a complete sentence.* My inner guide was helping me see that it was safe to say no. Twenty-four hours later I ended the deal.

We all have our own individual issues around using the word "no" as a complete sentence. A lot of the issues stem from people-pleasing behavior and the need to receive approval. Our work is to recognize that doing anything that's out of alignment with our core beliefs and truths will never work. As we come to accept this, we realize that no is often the most loving response.

Often people will resist your no's and manipulative folks will do whatever it takes to turn your no into a yes. Be mindful of these people and trust that the more you exercise the word "no" the more it will become second nature.

To begin this practice, take an inventory of the areas in your life in which you are saying yes when you really want to say no. Make a list of all the ways you avoid saying no and then clearly outline how it affects your relationships and happiness. Here are some questions to get you started:

- In what instances do I avoid saying no?

- How does this behavior affect me?

- How does this behavior affect the other people involved?

- How would it have helped me and the other people involved had I said no?

Now that you have more clarity, the next step is to begin exercising your no's. Much like all the tools in this book, this new behavior requires repetition. Rather than trying to figure out how to say no perfectly, just get into the habit even if it doesn't feel comfortable at first. Beginning the new behavior may feel awkward and scary. That's cool. Sometimes the best way to move through fear is just to take action. The more confident you get at saying no, the more people will thank you for it.

Miracle Message #90:

"'No' is a complete sentence." — Latham Thomas

#MiraclesNow

#91: MEDITATE FOR MEMORY.

Do you sometimes feel like your memory is shot? When you keep coming up blank, it's probably a result of stress or information overload. Sleep deprivation also hurts our memory. Given our 24/7 schedules, it's no wonder we often feel like we're literally losing our minds.

Though memory loss can be scary, it can also be quickly reversed. Stress is the primary cause of memory loss in healthy people. Therefore, reducing stress is the number-one way to boost your memory and brain health. The most effective way to ditch stress and regain your brainpower is to meditate. According to a study by researchers at the Benson-Henry Institute for Mind Body Medicine at Massachusetts General Hospital, meditation actually turns off the genes that are activated by stress, thereby strengthening your overall health and brain functioning.

Many Kundalini meditations are geared toward strengthening brain function. One meditation in particular is called Kirtan Kriya. According to numerous brain tests and scans, Kirtan Kriya has proven to have incredible effects on the brain. In one study, participants who meditated for 12 minutes a day for 8 weeks experienced improved mental clarity and up to 50 percent better memory.

In Sanskrit, *Kirtan* means "song," and in Kundalini yoga, *Kriya* is referred to as a specific set of movements. This Kriya is like a singing meditation. Kirtan Kriya

involves the repetition of four sounds: *Saa, Taa, Naa, Maa.*
This mantra is designed to uplift you.

- **Saa** means birth or infinity
- **Taa** means life
- **Naa** means death or completion
- **Maa** means rebirth

While saying the sounds, you also touch your thumb
to your index finger (saying *Saa*), thumb to middle finger
(saying *Taa*), thumb to the ring finger (saying *Naa*), and
thumb to the pinky finger (saying *Maa*).

Sit in an upright position on the floor or in a chair.
Rest your hands on your knees with palms facing upward.
Chant the syllables *Saa, Taa, Naa, Maa*—lengthen the
ending of each sound as you repeat them.

You practice this meditation in the following manner:

- Out loud for two minutes
- In a whisper for two minutes
- In silence for four minutes
- In a whisper for two more minutes
- Out loud for two more minutes

You can practice this for as little as 1 minute a day and
as many as 12 minutes. Practicing the Kirtan Kriya for 12
minutes a day can further improve cognition and activate
parts of the brain that are central to memory.

It's time to give our brains a break to recover from the
onslaught of stimuli. It's important to exercise our brains
the same way we exercise our physical muscles. Use this

Kriya if you feel like your brain is zapped and you need a reboot. If this works for you, test a 40-day practice and pay attention to your memory and overall motor skills.

Miracle Message #91:

It's important to exercise our brains
the same way we exercise our bodies.

#MiraclesNow

#92: GIVE YOURSELF PERMISSION TO FEEL.

Most of our issues and hang-ups stem from unprocessed feelings. Underneath every limiting belief, negative pattern, attack thought, and fear of the world lives a feeling that hasn't come to the surface for healing. Instead of feeling these feelings, we work hard to anesthetize them. We eat over our feelings, drink over them, work over them, use drugs over them, gossip over them, complain over them—and so on. In time these numbing-out techniques become addictions. Then we obsess about the addictive pattern rather than get to the root cause of the condition, which is the unexpressed pain.

In many cases people are not aware that they haven't been feeling their feelings. As a recovering drug addict, I experienced this firsthand. In my first year of sobriety, I felt feelings I never knew were there. For most of my adolescence, I'd used some type of addiction to cover up what I was so afraid to feel. Whether it was a romantic partner, my career, drugs, or alcohol, I was avoiding my feelings. Once I got clean, all I was left with were my feelings. It was intense to feel so much so fast—but it was also the greatest healing I've ever experienced. As a result of giving myself permission to feel my feelings, I was able to truly start living freely. I no longer had to lean on outside numbing devices to suppress feelings that I feared. I learned that it was safe to feel.

My coach, Rha Goddess, taught me that I could give myself permission to feel my feelings. Rha helped me recognize that underneath my addictive behavior was a feeling of fear and inadequacy. She helped me practice describing the feeling. With her guidance I was able to explain to her that the feeling was deep within my chest like a tight ball of gray yarn all tangled up. This description helped me greatly. Rha went on to teach me to feel that feeling in my chest whenever I noticed it arising. She suggested that if I felt the feeling for 90 seconds it could change naturally. She was right. Each time the feeling would come up my immediate response would be an urge to turn to an addictive pattern. Instead I chose to feel it fully and completely. In the presence of that honest feeling, I was able to allow it to pass through me naturally. I was finally free.

This practice changed my life forever. It taught me that my feelings from my past were safe to experience. After I truly honored them, I could release them. And once I was no longer afraid of feeling, I no longer had to run from my fear. I could just be present in the experience of the moment.

You, too, can be free from your negative patterns once you truly feel the feelings that dwell below them. Begin this practice right away. The next time you notice yourself caught up in a fearful experience or addictive pattern, take a moment to feel the feeling in your body. Describe it thoroughly (a tight steel knot in your stomach, an icy tightness in your jaw, a rumbling vibration in your chest) so you can clearly identify it when it arises. Then take 90 seconds to breathe in and out deeply and completely, allowing yourself to experience the feeling fully. Don't deny the feeling or push it down. Just be present with it. After 90 seconds witness the shift in your body, mind, and actions.

Practice this tool as often as possible and you'll experience miraculous change.

Miracle Message #92:

Feeling your feelings sets you free.

#MiraclesNow

#93: MEDITATE WITH A MALA.

At this point in the book, your miracle mind-set is on! With all these awesome techniques under your belt, it's likely that you're ready for some deep meditation. A fabulous tool for enhancing your meditation practice is a mala, which is a string of beads used for prayer. Each mala has 108 beads (in some cases they're made up of 54 or 27 beads, or another number divisible by nine). The beads are evenly spaced on silk thread, with a big bead (the guru bead) tying the mala, and a tassel attached to it. The tassel represents one thousand lotus petals.

Meditating with a mala can be a seriously groovy experience. This practice joins many of the Kundalini traditions into one meditation: Naad yoga (the recitation of sacred sounds), gemstone therapy, acupressure, and a deep contemplative meditation.

If you feel ready to deepen your meditation practice, begin incorporating a mala today. I'll guide you through it.

To begin, let's use a mantra you're familiar with: *Saa, Taa, Naa, Maa.* You can hold the mala in either hand at the bead that falls right after the guru bead. Then recite the mantra, *Saa, Taa, Naa, Maa,* while holding each bead between the thumb and one of the fingers, moving from one bead to the next with each sound. Pull each bead over the fingers with your thumb as you recite the mantra. Once you reach the guru bead, say a special prayer and begin again.

By placing different fingers underneath the beads you can stimulate meridian points that affect different parts of the brain. When you press the beads against the meridian point in your finger you can experience certain results. Each meridian is located on the side of each finger between the center point and the upper knuckle. Here's a breakdown of what each meridian point stimulates:

Index finger (Jupiter finger): Wisdom, knowledge, prosperity

Middle finger (Saturn finger): Patience

Ring finger (Sun finger): Health, vitality, a strong nervous system

Pinky (Mercury finger): Communication, intelligence

Choose the meridian point that you want to work on and begin your mala meditation today. Know that this meditation will help you deepen your spiritual awareness and heighten your capacity for stillness. Relax, focus, and enjoy!

Miracle Message #93:

Mala meditation deepens my awareness.

#MiraclesNow

#94: CONVERSE WITH THE UNIVERSE.

Yogi Bhajan said, "Prayer is talking to God. Meditation is letting God talk to you." As an adolescent caught in an existential crisis, I turned to meditation to release my fears and reconnect to peace. In the midst of drug addiction, I used meditation to find my way back to truth. Today as a Spirit Junkie I use meditation to receive inspiration and direction from God. Listening to God may seem like a trippy concept to some of you, especially if you're not religious or you've identified as an atheist. But as you know by now, I'm a big believer in the importance of everyone creating a God of their own understanding. I believe God is the divine force of love that lives within everything. That force can guide us and communicate through us when we are still. In stillness we can humbly receive Good Orderly Direction from our inner voice of love.

Spending time in stillness letting God talk to you can be your greatest source of strength in these tumultuous times. I can testify to the power of this path. By no means have I renounced the world to grow my spiritual practice. In fact, I've embraced the world fully. But to balance the wildness of the outer world we must activate our inner world. In this way we are led by love rather than our ego.

By now you're probably no longer a rookie when it comes to meditation. (If you are, that's cool. You can start practicing now.) It's likely you've meditated on a few occasions, and you may have established a regular practice using the meditations offered earlier in the book. So you understand what I'm saying when I tell you that one of the greatest ways to let love lead is through meditation. Following is a Kundalini meditation that will help us deepen our connection to God and strengthen our connection to our inner power. This practice is the meditation to know the experience of God. Here's how it goes:

Sit in Easy Pose with your spine straight.

Place your hands in your lap with the tip of each thumb touching each ring finger (this is the Surya mudra, as seen in the picture). Surya means "sun," and this mudra ignites energy, health, and intuition.

Breathe deeply at your own pace. Throughout this meditation, set the intention to communicate with the Universe. Welcome the voice of inspiration to flood through you.

It is suggested that you listen to the mantra "Rakhe Rakhanhar" while you sit in stillness. It offers protection against negative forces that might block your path, so you can communicate clearly with the Universe. You can download the song at Gabbyb.tv/Miracles-Now.

You can practice this meditation for as long as you wish, though it is suggested for 11 minutes. If it's hard for you to sit in stillness for this long, just begin with one minute and build up.

I have experienced many benefits from this meditation. It's given me a greater sense of intuition while speeding up synchronicity. The guidance I need to receive comes through more clearly. I practiced this meditation during a period when Mercury was in retrograde. This astrological phase can be difficult for communication, but by using this meditation I cut through confusion and clearly communicated my thoughts and desires.

Use this meditation to heighten your communication with the Universe, your inner guidance system, and the world.

Miracle Message #94:

"Prayer is talking to God. Meditation is letting God talk to you." — Yogi Bhajan

#YogiBhajan #MiraclesNow

#95: YOU DON'T NEED TO FIND YOUR PURPOSE. YOUR PURPOSE WILL FIND YOU.

I often hear people complain that they don't know what their purpose is. They feel confused, disconnected, and ungrounded. Sound familiar? It can be frustrating to wake up every day feeling purposeless. In many cases I see people pushing and controlling their actions to show themselves and the world that they are worthy, powerful, and helpful. The ego makes us think that our purpose is outside of ourselves, hidden behind a credential, a job title, or an altruistic mission. The outside search for purpose can lead to a lot of inner turmoil. When we seek external signifiers of purpose, we often end up feeling hollow or disappointed.

I've come to understand that you don't actually go out and find your purpose. Instead, your purpose is meant to find you. When we follow a spiritual path and peel back the layers of ego we've built against our inner truth, we begin to find what we've been looking for. We discover what is truthful and real to us. In that space of truth we begin to receive guidance. Some people are guided to serve the world through their careers. Some people are guided to bring children into the world. Others are guided to radical acts of forgiveness. It doesn't matter which action you're guided to; all that matters is that in some way your intention is to bring more love to the world. When you lead from a place of love, then you're living in your purpose.

The next time you get hung up on the idea that you need to "find your purpose," simply remind yourself that you don't need to find anything. Stay on your spiritual path and trust that your purpose is finding you. Trust that spiritual growth and inner awareness are all you need to be given. The Good Orderly Direction is moving toward the loving purpose of your life. Be patient and committed to living in love and leading from truth.

Miracle Message #95:

You don't need to find your purpose. Your purpose will find you.

#MiraclesNow

#96: YOUR EYES WILL SEE WHAT YOU DESIRE.

Each exercise in this book is designed to help you re-calibrate your energy and reframe your thoughts so that the Universe can then reorganize your life. You may not be fully comfortable with the belief that your thoughts and energy create your reality. However, if you've been taking these principles seriously, you're likely experiencing positive inner and outer shifts. Each shift is a miracle. Let these subtle shifts inspire you to have more faith in the power of your desires.

With your newfound understanding of how your thoughts and energy can affect your life, it's time to start co-creating your reality. The more you understand how energy works, the easier it is to change your circumstances in an instant. For example, I was in a cab with a friend one morning. I was heading uptown for a meeting and she was off to work. I could sense her energy was low and she seemed somewhat depressed. Her low vibe was bringing me down, too. When I asked her what was wrong, she explained that she felt down about having to go to work. She was irritated by the summer heat and her seemingly endless to-do list. I then asked her if she'd like to reframe her experience and try to change her mood. She gave me half a smile and said, "Yes, please." I helped her see how blessed she was and focus on everything that she had going for her. In one minute, she thought her way out of a negative attitude and reenergized herself.

Later that day I got a text from my friend saying, "Thank you for saving my day!" I replied, "Your eyes will see what you desire." This gentle reminder is something that we can all use more often. We often experience what we want to experience, regardless of our outside circumstances. In my friend's case, nothing outside changed. It was still hot out, her to-do list was still long, and she was still on her way to work. All that changed was her desire to see happiness instead of negativity. That was a miracle.

At this point in your miracle-worker practice, you're prepared to proactively create more shifts in your life. Start now. What are you thinking? What are you feeling? And how are your thoughts and feelings affecting your current situation? If your thoughts and energy are positive, ask yourself how you can make them even more awesome. If your thoughts and energy are affecting you negatively, begin the reframing process. Desire something different. Choose to see the positive, focus on gratitude, and open up a new perspective. Whenever you catch yourself caught up in a negative story, do this reframing exercise for yourself. Redirect your thoughts to what is working, what is positive, and what is flowing in your life. When you focus on the flow, you will flow with it.

Take responsibility for your own happiness. Doing so is a gift you give yourself and everyone around you. The happier you are, the more positivity you bring to the world.

Miracle Message #96:
Your eyes will see what you desire.
#MiraclesNow

#97: BREATHE LIKE A DOG AND BOOST YOUR IMMUNE SYSTEM.

Did the title get your attention? You might be laughing at the mental image of a panting Labrador, but I promise this is no joke. I'm going to introduce you to a powerful Kundalini meditation that will help boost your immune system by breathing like a dog. It is your responsibility to take care of your immune system so that you can enjoy life and share your joy with the world. Practice this meditation when you feel your constitution weakening, or practice it every day to maintain your overall health.

Here's how it works.

Sit in Easy Pose with your chin and your chest pressed out. Stick out your tongue all the way and breathe rapidly through your mouth, keeping your tongue out the entire time. This is called Dog Breath. Practice this breath for three to five minutes.

To finish the meditation inhale and hold your breath for 15 seconds as you press your tongue hard against the upper palate. Repeat the closing breath two more times.

This is a powerful exercise. When you feel a tingling in your toes, thighs, and lower back, it's a sure sign that you're doing it correctly.

Your health is vital to your happiness and fulfillment. Use this meditation to ward off infection and to maintain a strong immune system.

Miracle Message #97:

Your health is vital to your happiness and fulfillment.
#MiraclesNow

#98: RESTRAIN YOUR PEN AND TONGUE.

Ever have one of those moments in which you wish you could erase an e-mail you just sent or rewind a conversation you just had? Whenever we react too quickly we cut off the connection to our inner guidance system and react from a place of ego. Whether we're responding with a nasty attitude, angrily reacting, or simply saying too much, it's never a good idea to respond quickly.

Bill Wilson, the co-founder of Alcoholics Anonymous, said, "Nothing pays off like restraint of pen and tongue." His suggestion saved me on countless occasions. I used to be very reactive, which never worked out well for me. Inevitably, responding based on my first impulse led to a sense of regret and further complicated whatever issue I was dealing with. Though it was difficult at first, learning restraint of pen and tongue became a blessing in my life and saved me from many unnecessary problems.

If you tend to be reactive, too, I suggest you test this tool. The next time you want to quickly react to a situation, take three long, deep breaths. Use your yogic breath and deeply breathe into your diaphragm, expanding the back of your rib cage. On the exhale, allow your diaphragm to contract. Taking a few moments to focus on your breath allows the emotional charge fueling that fired-up reaction to fade, thereby clearing your mind. Once you're done with the three breaths, ask yourself, *What is a more loving response?* Take a moment to allow your inspiration to speak and guide you. In an instant you can receive higher guidance that can save you from a lot of unnecessary and unpleasant issues. Once you've moved through the personal intervention, say to yourself, *I choose to exercise restraint of pen and tongue.*

Miracle Message #98:

"Nothing pays off like restraint of pen and tongue."
— Bill Wilson

#MiraclesNow

#99: STOP OBSESSING.

It's easy to flip out when your carefully planned agenda goes awry. The ego gets attached to certain outcomes and circumstances: It desperately wants your relationship to last, your job to remain forever secure—it even gets hung up on something as mundane as the sun shining, which means a cloudy day can ruin everything. The ego tries to control all outcomes regardless of how powerless you are over them. This need to control is a major stressor in life and will affect your well-being and happiness.

Some people are so consumed with controlling outcomes that their obsessive thoughts become paralyzing. For instance, some obsess about travel plans months before a trip. Others freak out about the outcome of a relationship even as it's going well. As I'm a recovering obsessive, I'm all too familiar with this pattern. I used to obsess to the point of exhaustion. I was living in a constant state of faithlessness. I believed that if I didn't control a situation, it would never work out the way I wanted. Ironically, all my controlling behavior actually got in the way of my desired outcomes. My energy was frantic, controlling, and fearful. If you're someone who spends your days (and nights—we can obsess in our dreams, too) obsessing over outcomes, it's time to redirect your energy.

When we're overly controlling, we're out of alignment with our spirits and focused only on what we can do as individual bodies. The reason we try to control outcomes is because we're afraid that if we don't make it happen no one will.

When this feeling comes over you, it's a sure sign that you do not trust the energy of the Universe. Each exercise in this book has in some way guided you to tap into the ever-present energy of the Universe, the energy that supports your every move. That energy can be tapped into through intentions, prayer, meditation, and service-minded actions. That energy is your true power when you feel powerless. The key to releasing your need to control is to accept that there is a power greater than you working on your behalf to support you. The next step is to mindfully tap into that power through your thoughts, prayers, and intentions.

To get you back into the groove of Universal energy, let's practice an awesome tool that will help you surrender your need to control: Make a list of all of the things you're trying to control. Next to each issue write: *I am powerless over this situation and I surrender it to the Universe.* Carry this list around with you. Whenever you notice yourself obsessing, bust out your list as a reminder of your powerlessness and the opportunity to surrender. Let me be clear: I am not suggesting that you do not have dominion over your own actions. But once you have made your move, it's time to surrender the outcome. Lean on the list as often as possible as a tool for shifting your energy in the moment. A simple intention to surrender your control is all you need to experience miracles.

Miracle Message #99:

The simple intention to surrender control
is all you need to experience miracles.

#MiraclesNow

#100: ENERGIZE WHEN YOU'RE SHORT ON SLEEP.

In earlier exercises I shared how I believe sleep is a spiritual practice. Given the busyness of life, sometimes we can't get the amount of sleep that our body truly needs. On a book tour, I typically function each day on a half-night's sleep. Therefore, I've had to find tools for recalibrating my energy to stay alert, inspired, and vibrant. When I was on the *May Cause Miracles* tour, I used an incredible Kundalini asana (yoga posture) as a sleep substitute. Yogi Bhajan taught that doing a shoulder stand for fifteen minutes can equal two hours of sleep because it relaxes you so deeply. Though a shoulder stand is not a long-term replacement for sleep, it can be a great substitute when you just can't catch enough Z's.

To do a shoulder stand, lie on your back and bring your spine and legs up to a vertical position, supporting your butt with your arms. Your shoulders and elbows support your body weight (get your legs as vertical as you can and make sure that all of your weight is on your shoulders, not on your neck). If a shoulder stand is difficult for you, do an easier inversion. Place a bolster or two thick folded blankets under your lower back, put your legs up straight, and prop them against the wall. Rest in either of these positions for as long as you can, breathing deeply in and out of your nose. Try it for a minute and then build up to 15.

If you have trouble falling asleep at night, I have another Kundalini tool that's helped me greatly. Once you're lying on your back in bed, keep your heels on the bed as you breathe deep long breaths through your nose. On the inhale, stretch your toes toward your head while you chant in your mind, *Sat.* On the exhale, point your toes and mentally chant, *Nam.* Continue this practice for three minutes. After a few minutes, you'll fall right asleep.

Miracle Message #100:

Fifteen minutes of shoulder stand equals two hours of sleep.

#YogiBhajan #MiraclesNow

#101: LIVE IN A JUDGMENT-FREE ZONE.

Have you ever gone a day without judgment? I for one cannot say that I have. Though I don't consider myself a judgmental person, I catch myself judging all throughout the day—myself, people I know, people I don't know, and so on. *A Course in Miracles* says, "The ego cannot survive without judgment."

Judgment creates separation. From the *Course*'s perspective, separation occurs when we disconnect from oneness. Judgment reinforces the illusion that we are separate from others, and that separation makes us feel more or less special than others. These special illusions create negativity within relationships. When we judge ourselves, we imply that we're less than others—inferior in some (or every) way. When we judge others, we suggest that they're "less than." Judgment and separation make us feel terrible. We feel isolated, competitive, and distrustful. We pour a lot of time and energy into comparing and attacking. Worst of all, judgment breeds more judgment to keep the illusion of separation alive. It's a vicious cycle.

The *Course* says, "The ego seeks to divide and separate. Spirit seeks to unify and heal." Though judgment may be our default, unity is our truth. The moment we release judgment, unity is restored. Each shift from judgment to unity is a miracle.

The pattern of judgment will not be removed immediately. I still struggle with it daily even though it's the
opposite of what I believe. Your commitment to see love
is all that matters. With your desire to reconnect to the
truth within, you can begin by using an affirmation from
the *Course* workbook. Each time you catch yourself judging others or yourself, simply say, "I can escape from the
world I see by giving up attack thoughts." This affirmation
is a reminder that when you release an attack thought, you
can immediately reconnect with love. Use this practice
daily and let it become a new pattern to choose love over
judgment.

Miracle Message #101:

"I can escape from the world I see by giving up attack thoughts."

#ACIM #MiraclesNow

#102: WHEN IN DOUBT, PLAY IT OUT.

Changing a bad habit can be tough at first. Real change requires commitment and repetition of a new behavior. While in the process of adopting a new behavior, we'll have many moments when our ego will try to talk us out of it. For instance, in my first year off coffee I struggled each time I walked past a café and inhaled the scent of fresh beans and brews. The daily temptations led me to many moments in which I contemplated buying a steaming cup. My addiction to coffee far outweighed my willpower.

Eventually the desire to pick up a cup of coffee became so strong that I found myself seconds away from relapsing. In order to protect myself from falling back into a pattern that did not serve me, I used a technique to think my way back to sanity. When I caught myself about to walk into the coffee shop, I played out the situation. First I saw myself drinking the coffee. Then I saw myself get so wired from the caffeine that I'd barely be able to communicate with people because I would be feeling so manic. Next I fast-forwarded ahead another half an hour to my post-caffeine crash. My energy would have tanked and I would be catatonic for the rest of the day. In addition, my stomach would hurt, my head would ache, and I would be completely unproductive. This was a typical day for me when I drank coffee. So playing out the scene was easy because it was all too familiar. After three minutes of visualizing the unpleasant sequence of events, I could easily walk away from the coffee shop and head straight to the juice bar instead.

Our ego is a shrewd eraser of the truth behind why we make positive change. That's why it's so easy to fall back into old behaviors. We start to give ourselves permission to go backward and we lose sight of why we stopped in the first place. Playing it out will greatly serve you when you're about to fall back into old behavior. Maybe you're about to mix a drink after 90 days of sobriety, or maybe you're about to text the lover who you know is really wrong for you. Whatever the issue, whenever you're in doubt, play it out. Think your way through the entire story. Not just the fun part where you get high on caffeine or buzzed from a beer. Play the story all the way through to the end when you crash and burn. Your honesty and willingness to remember what is real will save you when you want to relapse.

Miracle Message #102:

When in doubt, play it out.

#MiraclesNow

#103: HOW WOULD YOU LIVE IF YOU KNEW YOU WERE BEING GUIDED?

So much of the anxiety, stress, and turmoil we experience comes from our lack of faith in the Universe. We believe that we need to make everything happen and plan every detail to feel safe. We live our lives controlled by outcomes and future plans. In fleeting moments we reconnect with the flow of the Universe, such as when we're feeling serene on a meditation pillow, gazing at a still lake in the midst of a walk, or sweating it out in a yoga class. Fleeting moments of connection remind us of our truth. But what would life be like if we always remembered that we were being guided? How different would we be?

For this exercise, I suggest that you create a vision statement. At the top of the page in a notebook, write: *What would my life be like if I knew I was always being guided?* Then spend five minutes on your answer. Set a timer and free associate. Let go of all your fears and small-minded thoughts. Surrender to your creative thoughts and imagine what life would be like if you knew you were being guided. Let your pen flow.

When the timer beeps, read what you wrote and breathe in the feelings that come up as you read. Are there feelings of disbelief? Or do you feel an intuitive sense that this is how life should be? If you're feeling even the slightest sense of peace after reading your vision statement, then you're tapping into your truth. There is a place within each of us that truly believes that we are being guided. Each moment of the day, the ego works hard to keep us disconnected from that truth. It's our job to unlearn the ego's fear and remember our faithful truth.

Let your vision statement remind you that you *are* always being guided—even when times are tough. In the moments when you cannot possibly see a positive outcome to the experience you're having, it's imperative that you trust in the Universe. Your trust and faith offer you an opportunity to learn, grow, and heal. Often we see difficult times as punishment from the Universe or we decide to lose our faith in God and love altogether. When times are tough, we need faith more than ever. Maybe you're going through a divorce, living with a health condition, or struggling with a difficult decision. No matter your circumstances, you can decide now to believe you are guided at all times. When you accept this, you can truly live happy and free. Genuine freedom comes from knowing the Universe has your back.

Use what you wrote as a freedom statement that you can turn to whenever you're in doubt. It is a strong reminder of your connection to the Universe and the energy presence that is always supporting you.

Miracle Message #103:

Your happiness can be measured by the level of your faith in love.

#MiraclesNow

#104: FACE THE TRUTH.

No matter how hard we try to avoid the truth, the Universe will always show us what's real. My dear friend Danielle says, "We may not want to face the truth, but we can't be on a spiritual path and not have the truth be in our face." Danielle is right. When we embark on a spiritual journey we become more aware of what it feels like to avoid the truth.

The truth will always come forward, and fast. In these times, when energy has sped up and technology exposes everything, little remains hidden. Before we started our spiritual journey, dwelling in the lies of the ego may have felt strangely safe, almost cozy. But once we're committed to the journey, that space becomes ever more uncomfortable and restrictive.

I see a lot of people on spiritual paths who are open to exposing their truth in some areas of life, but unwilling to surrender others. This won't work. We must be willing to face the truth in all situations, not just those that are convenient. The corners of our lives that remain in darkness need to be brought to the light so we can fully develop into the powerful beings we are meant to be.

This book has helped you begin the journey of exposing those dark corners to get honest about what is real to you. At this point in your practice, it's time to dive even deeper into your truth. Revisit the journey you've taken with this book. What came up for you? What have you learned about yourself? What are you still avoiding? Take a few moments to reflect. Then, with all the honesty you

can muster, write down the areas where you're still denying the truth. It might make you cringe; it might make
your heart beat faster; or it might even freak you out.
That's okay: Honesty takes courage.

Your honesty is imperative to further your growth
and happiness. It may be scary to look at what you've
been hiding. But these days I find it much scarier not to
look. Trust that if you were called to this book, at this time,
then you've received an invitation to live more, feel more,
and serve more. That invitation requires that you honestly
move through anything that is holding you back from
stepping in fully.

Now is the perfect time to reenergize your commitment to your practice. Amma, the hugging saint, said,
"When an eggshell cracks from the outside it's crushed.
When it cracks from the inside a being is born." Be willing to crack open from the inside. Set a new intention to
get honest about the areas of your life that your ego still
runs. Accept that being on a spiritual path means surrendering *it all*, not just the areas that are easy to release.

The time to step in fully and surrender more is now.
Forgive the parent you've been resenting. Address your
addiction. Face your darkest fear. Go big and go home to
the truth that is you.

Miracle Message #104:

Face your truth or your truth
will be put back in your face.

#MiraclesNow

#105: TRUE ABUNDANCE
IS AN INSIDE JOB.

Financial fear and insecurity have been soaring for the past few years. With all the negative reports on the economy, it's easy to get hooked into the mentality of lack. Focusing on lack creates more lack—a truly vicious cycle—while dwelling in abundance creates more abundance.

Whatever we think about money leads to how we feel about money. That feeling gives off an energy that either supports our earning capacity or hurts it. Energy is currency. If we want to use our energy to earn more and have financial freedom, we need to clean up our thoughts and beliefs.

We start clearing the blocks by becoming conscious of them. There are three big blocks when it comes to abundance. One is the lack mentality: the belief that there will never be enough. People who languish in this lack mentality are convinced that they'll never achieve abundance and will constantly struggle to feel secure. The second major block is the belief that having a certain amount of money makes you "better than." People who place importance on money see themselves as not good enough or "less than" if they don't have a lot—and those that do have a lot can't enjoy it because they fear losing it or because they have less than someone else. The final way fear blocks our earning capacity is through the belief that there's not enough to go around—that only a certain number of people get to experience abundance; that there's a limit to it.

Throughout the day, witness your thoughts, energy, and behavior around money. When you notice a fearful thought around money, use the moment to create a perceptual shift. Immediately forgive yourself for having that thought and choose to see it differently. Maybe you catch yourself staring wistfully in a boutique window, thinking, "I wish I could afford a great pair of boots." Right away, choose a new thought—such as, "I am grateful for what I *do* have and I choose not to focus on my lack." This simple shift can redirect your energy and amp up your gratitude and positivity. Suddenly, you might see the latte you're sipping in a whole new light, or remember that you actually really like the shoes you've got on.

Your true abundance starts with your belief system. Marie Forleo, founder of Rich Happy & Hot B-School, says, "Commit to clean up your beliefs and behavior around money and you'll be on your way to enjoying a truly rich life, inside and out."

Miracle Message #105:
True abundance is an inside job.
#MiraclesNow

#106: REPEATING NEW BEHAVIOR CREATES PERMANENT CHANGE.

You now have a toolbox of more than 100 techniques for zapping stress, shifting your mood, and achieving peace. These tools are forever in your back pocket to grab when you need them. To take your practice even further, let's go deeper with one of the exercises so that it can become second nature. Sustainable change comes from discipline, commitment, and repetition.

Remember, Yogi Bhajan said that 90 percent of the work is just showing up. For this principle, take your time to wholeheartedly show up for an exercise that inspired you. Take a moment to review each exercise and then pick the one that you need most right now. Not the one that seems the easiest or the most convenient to do—the exercise you truly need right now. Then set the intention to practice the exercise consistently for the next 40 days. If you fall off the wagon, begin again at day one.

Give yourself the opportunity to soak up the practice. Sink into it and let it envelop you. Let the tool take over as you use the repetition as a guide to creating permanent change. In 40 days you can reroute the neural pathways in your brain to create permanent change. Yogi Bhajan said that practicing every day for 40 days straight will break any negative habits that block you from expansion.

If you feel called to take your exercise even further, you can continue the repetition. Yogi Bhajan also said that practicing for 90 days establishes a new habit in your conscious and subconscious. It changes you in a very deep way. Practice every day for 120 days straight and you will confirm the new habit. Practice every day for 1,000 days straight and you will master the practice.

With repetition you establish a deep connection to the practice. No matter the challenges you face, you can turn to your practice for help at any time.

Yogi Bhajan taught that a habit is a subconscious chain reaction between the mind, the glandular system, and the nervous system. Our most deep-rooted habits are developed at a very young age. Some of them serve you and some of them don't. By doing a 40-, 90-, 120-, or 1,000-day practice, you can rewire that chain reaction and develop new and powerful habits that serve your highest good.

Miracle Message #106:

You can develop new and powerful habits that serve your highest good.

#MiraclesNow

#107: "TO TEACH IS TO LEARN."

As a spiritual student, I believe that we sign an invisible oath to be a teacher in some way. As we expand our inner awareness and bear witness to our lives as they blossom, we likely sense the desire to spread the love. When we share our spiritual gifts, they grow. *A Course in Miracles* says, "To teach is to learn." As a teacher of the *Course*, I can testify to this truth. I have witnessed my spiritual awareness and faith grow immensely from my commitment to being a teacher.

Early in my *Course* studies, I read about how the students show up when the teacher is ready. This was the case for me. As soon as I made the commitment to share the information I was learning, my students began appearing. They showed up as mentees, family members, and, in my case, audience members, as I began to share the messages through lectures and videos. When you're on a spiritual path, teaching comes naturally. You don't need to figure out who to teach or where to go. Rather, you remain a humble student with the willingness to share the beautiful gifts you've been given.

At points in my spiritual journey when I decided to learn more, I was guided to teach more. For instance, before I found Kundalini yoga and meditation, I felt a strong call to heighten my own practice. Though I'd been a spiritual teacher for seven years, I was seeking a more visceral experience of spirit. I prayed to know more. Quickly my prayers were answered when I was invited to a private

Kundalini class hosted by a dear friend. I didn't even like yoga, but there was a voice within me saying, *Get your ass into that class.* From the moment I met my teacher, Gurmukh, and experienced the technology of Kundalini, I knew I was not only meant to be a dedicated student, but I was meant to be a teacher.

With one month of Kundalini classes under my belt, I started saying out loud (to everyone, including my lecture audiences) that I was going to become a Kundalini teacher. I had no idea where this proclamation was coming from. Spirit was speaking through me, holding me accountable as I stated my commitment to thousands of people in lecture halls and the Twittersphere. I was being called to teach.

Then, one afternoon in Kundalini class, I kept hearing my inner voice say, *It's time to teach, it's time to teach.* Immediately following the class, I thanked the teacher. She looked at me and said, "Gabrielle, I'm familiar with your work. I think you should teach Kundalini." I smiled and accepted the Universal memo. Twenty-four hours later I signed up for 270 hours of Kundalini yoga and meditation teacher training.

Becoming a spiritual teacher isn't our choice. It's an unconscious commitment we make with the Universe. It's not something that we do; it's something that happens to us. We can all teach in our own unique ways. You don't need to be a self-help book author and motivational speaker to be a spiritual teacher. You just need to be a spiritual student with a desire to serve. Yogi Bhajan said, "If you want to learn something, read about it. If you want to understand something, write about it. If you want to master something, teach it." You've made it this far and it's likely you're hearing your own call to teach. Don't deny that inner voice. Don't push it away with limiting beliefs like, "I'm not ready for that teacher training," or "Who am I to share these tools?" That's all a bunch of crap. When you make the decision to share your gifts, spirit will give you all that you need to facilitate the process.

The principles in this book are designed to be shared because the world desperately needs more light. When you are called to share the spiritual awareness you now have, don't hesitate to speak up. Be the lighthouse. In your light, others will become illuminated.

A Course in Miracles teaches us, "A miracle is a service. It is the maximal service you can render to another. It is a way of loving your neighbor as yourself. You recognize your own and your neighbor's worth simultaneously." We need more miracle workers to balance the energy of these times. We need you.

Miracle Message #107:

"To learn something, read about it.
To understand something, write about it.
To master something, teach it." — Yogi Bhajan

#YogiBhajan #MiraclesNow

#108: YOU ARE THE GURU.

We've come quite far on this journey. By now you may feel well equipped to handle difficult areas of your life, to move through stress, and to offer guidance to people in need. With your new toolbox, you can experience life with more grace, peace, and freedom from fear. This is a miracle.

There will still be many moments of self-doubt and self-sabotage. There will be resisters from the outside world and ego backlash from your inner world. There will be obstacles that will attempt to block you from your faith in love.

These obstacles can take you down or they can lift you up. It depends on how you choose to perceive them. If you face obstacles with a miracle mind-set, you will find opportunities for growth rather than blocks on your path. If you continue to trust your inner guidance system, you will always be led in the right direction. Accept that the guidance you need is within you.

You are the guru, and it's time to own it. Yes, you'll continue to be guided to teachers and healers who will help you strengthen your miracle muscles, but the true direction must come from within.

Jesus said:

If you bring forth what is within you,

what you bring forth will save you.

If you do not bring forth what is within you,

what you do not bring forth will destroy you.

This has been a journey of unlearning the fears from the past and reclaiming the loving truth within. As you continue to apply these principles in your life, the voice of love soon will become the only voice you hear. The voice of love will never leave you.

Use this book for the rest of your life. Whenever you're stuck, open the book to any page and trust that your inner guide has led you to the perfect exercise. Have faith that the pages you open to will reflect back exactly what you need at that time. Trust in the guidance and then take action.

Trust that you have all the answers, all the resources, and all the knowledge to show up for this life with magnitude and strength. Unleash your inner power with the conviction of a saint. Know that you are the guru.

Miracle Message #108:

You are the guru.

#MiraclesNow

The Beginning . . .

Acknowledgments

There are many people who helped bring this book into the world. First I want to thank my agent, Michele Martin. You are my literary partner, and it is an honor to walk through this life connected to you. To Louise Hay, Reid Tracy, Patty Gift, and the entire Hay House team, it is wonderful to be part of your publishing family. Thank you all for your hard work on this book. To Kelly Wolf and my amazing PR team at Sarah Hall PR, thank you for helping me share this book with the world. I thank my editor, Katie Karlson, for bringing her magic to each of my books. A special thanks to the design team who created the cover and interior shots: Chloe Crespi, Emily French, Michael O'Neill, and Katrina Sorrentino.

To my husband, Zach, thank you for always believing in me and holding the space for me to share this work with the world.

Finally, I'd like to thank Yogi Bhajan and the Golden Bridge Yoga community for helping me become a stronger teacher and expanding my inner awareness.

Sat Nam

About the Author

Gabrielle Bernstein is the *New York Times* best-selling author of *May Cause Miracles*. She appears regularly as an expert on NBC's *Today* show, has been featured on Oprah's *Super Soul Sunday* as a next-generation thought leader, and was named "a new role model" by *The New York Times*. She is also the author of the books *Add More ~ing to Your Life* and *Spirit Junkie*. Gabrielle is the founder HerFuture.com, a social networking site for women to inspire, empower, and connect.

Gabrielle was chosen as one of 16 YouTube Next Video Bloggers, she was named one of Mashable's 11 Must-Follow Twitter Accounts for Inspiration, and she was featured on the Forbes List of 20 Best Branded Women. Gabrielle has a monthly segment on the *Today* show and a weekly radio show on Hay House Radio. She has been featured in media outlets such as *The New York Times Sunday Styles, ELLE, OWN, Kathy Lee & Hoda, Oprah Radio, Anderson Live, Access Hollywood, Marie Claire, Health, SELF, Women's Health, Glamour, The New York Times Thursday Styles, Sunday Times UK*, and many more. She was also featured on the covers of *Experience Life* and *Self-Made Magazine* (top 50 Women in Business).

Hay House Titles of Related Interest

YOU CAN HEAL YOUR LIFE, the movie,
starring Louise Hay & Friends
(available as a 1-DVD program and an expanded 2-DVD set)
Watch the trailer at: www.LouiseHayMovie.com

THE SHIFT, the movie, starring Dr. Wayne W. Dyer
(available as a 1-DVD program and an expanded 2-DVD set)
Watch the trailer at: www.DyerMovie.com

🌿 🌿

REVEAL: A Sacred Manual for Getting Spiritually Naked,
by Meggan Watterson

*THE TAPPING SOLUTION: A Revolutionary System for
Stress-Free Living,* by Nick Ortner

LOVEABILITY: Knowing How to Love and Be Loved,
by Robert Holden, Ph.D.

*E-SQUARED: Nine Do-It-Yourself Energy Experiments that
Prove Your Thoughts Create Your Reality,* by Pam Grout

All of the above are available at your local bookstore,
or may be ordered by contacting Hay House (see next page).

🌿 🌿

We hope you enjoyed this Hay House book. If you'd like to receive our online catalog featuring additional information on Hay House books and products, or if you'd like to find out more about the Hay Foundation, please contact:

Hay House, Inc., P.O. Box 5100, Carlsbad, CA 92018-5100
(760) 431-7695 or (800) 654-5126
(760) 431-6948 (fax) or (800) 650-5115 (fax)
www.hayhouse.com® • www.hayfoundation.org

※ ※

Published and distributed in Australia by:
Hay House Australia Pty. Ltd., 18/36 Ralph St., Alexandria NSW 2015
Phone: 612-9669-4299 • *Fax:* 612-9669-4144 • www.hayhouse.com.au

Published and distributed in the United Kingdom by: Hay House UK, Ltd.,
Astley House, 33 Notting Hill Gate, London W11 3JQ
Phone: 44-20-3675-2450 • *Fax:* 44-20-3675-2451 • www.hayhouse.co.uk

Published and distributed in the Republic of South Africa by:
Hay House SA (Pty), Ltd., P.O. Box 990, Witkoppen 2068
Phone/Fax: 27-11-467-8904 • www.hayhouse.co.za

Published in India by: Hay House Publishers India,
Muskaan Complex, Plot No. 3, B-2, Vasant Kunj, New Delhi 110 070
Phone: 91-11-4176-1620 • *Fax:* 91-11-4176-1630 • www.hayhouse.co.in

Distributed in Canada by: Raincoast Books,
2440 Viking Way, Richmond, B.C. V6V 1N2
Phone: 1-800-663-5714 • *Fax:* 1-800-565-3770 • www.raincoast.com

※ ※

Take Your Soul on a Vacation

Visit www.HealYourLife.com® to regroup, recharge,
and reconnect with your own magnificence.
Featuring blogs, mind-body spirit news, and
life-changing wisdom from Louise Hay and friends.

Visit www.HealYourLife.com today!